THE RATIONAL AND SOCIAL

FOUNDATIONS OF MUSIC

THE RATIONAL AND SOCIAL

FOUNDATIONS OF MUSIC

BY *Max Weber*

Translated and Edited by

DON MARTINDALE

JOHANNES RIEDEL

GERTRUDE NEUWIRTH

 SOUTHERN ILLINOIS UNIVERSITY PRESS 1958

PRINTED IN THE UNITED STATES OF AMERICA BY

AMERICAN BOOK–STRATFORD PRESS, INC., NEW YORK

DESIGNED BY ANDOR BRAUN

Prefatory Note

IN THE stereotypes of an older generation, music belongs among the spiritual activities of man. In a world that thought in terms of contrasts between the sacred and the secular, the spiritual and the material, this terminology was directly appropriate. For in his music (and other arts) man's activity assumes the properties of intensity without practical purpose, discipline without externally imposed restrictions. No wonder that in the arts one often feels that he is in the realm of the pure spirit with its spontaneous activity and self-imposed rules rising, at times, to lyrical self-expression.

In the same society where music is produced and enjoyed, the patterned, infinitely varied strategies of social life unfold in customs and conventions hardening into institutions or melting into fads and fashions.

Moralists and politicians, humanists and religious neophytes have seen that these two spheres, the artistic and the everyday, have some relation to one another. The moralist would denounce it; the politician use it; the humanist affirm it; the religious neophyte withdraw from it. Some of these attitudes even reappear in the booster and the social critic.

The modern sociology of music is the disciplined contemporary form of the inquiry into the relation between music and society. The study by Max Weber, one of the greatest sociologists of the twentieth century, of the rational and social foundations of music is a pioneering venture of the modern discipline. Though it is a quarter of a century since Max Weber's essay appeared (first published in 1921), interest in Weber and the sociology of music has continued to grow. Johannes Riedel was asked to give a paper on Weber's sociology of music at Jordan College, Indianapolis, Indiana, on April 28, 1956, to a section of the Midwest Chapter of the American Musicological Society. We take this as one among many such evidences that a translation of the Weber essay is long overdue.

Don Martindale

Gertrude Neuwirth

Johannes Riedel

October, 1957

CONTENTS

INTRODUCTION

MAX WEBER'S SOCIOLOGY

OF MUSIC

THE STUDY of the interrelations between society and music is not to be undertaken carelessly nor is it one affording easy solutions. Since the patterns of music production and appreciation may change while the society remains constant and the same music may be received and loved by the people of quite different societies, there is no one-to-one casual interdetermination of society and music. One must reject as vulgar errors the Nazi idea that there is a true Aryan music and the Communist idea that Western music is of a decadent bourgeois type. The sociology of music could not mean this, for it would need be rejected out of hand.

However, it is a matter of familiar observation that there are close ties between various social elements and music. The musician is a member of society like anyone else. His requirement for making a living may be bound up with his artistic role. If he earns a livelihood independently of his art, his music has the form of a hobby or leisure-time pursuit. The manner in which he cultivates his talents will tend to differ from that of the musician who makes a living by means of his art. The musician requires an audience. His product is molded by the demand or lack of demand for his art. In his art the musician employs instruments related to the level of technology of his civilization. His finest performances may be attended for status rather than aesthetic reasons as occasions for the better elements of society to see and be seen by each other in appropriate dress, jewelry, furs. The artist may be a free agent producing his wares in open competition with others. He may be a kept and pampered object, as much a part of an elegant household as a combed and brushed poodle. It is a matter of familiar observation that all such factors enter as encouragements and discouragements in the production and consumption of music.

Thus, there is a kind of common-sense sociology of music familiar to us all. We know that, generally, fine art is for fine people and vulgar art is for the not so fine. We know that status factors affect the change in artistic styles. We know that artistic performances have extramusical functions. The sociology of music takes its point of departure from such familiar observations. It explores the boundaries between the sciences of sociology and musicology, attempting to explain those links between society and music that common observation reveals.

Max Weber's pioneering essay, "The Rational and Social Foundations of Music," [1] has special interest to both sociologists and musicians, for it cuts below the surface of a common-sense sociology of music to fundamental issues. Weber attempted to trace the influence of social factors on the very creative core and technical basis of music. In its broadest sense, Weber's thesis was that Western music has peculiar rational properties produced by social factors in Occidental development. Right or wrong,

Weber's thesis assumes a relevance for the deepest levels of musical theory. It also forms a test case as to the values of sociological and musicological sciences for each other.

As one of the great sociologists in modern times, Max Weber is universally known among social scientists. Inasmuch as he is much less widely known in musical circles, it will be useful for some of our readers briefly to review those aspects of his thought relevant to his sociology of music.

Basic Sociological Ideas

Max Weber (1864–1920) was born in Berlin of an upper middle-class family. His father was a prominent figure in the National Liberal Party of the Bismarckian era, serving for some years in the Reichstag. Weber was entered upon the study of law, his father's profession. His first academic appointment was that of *Privatdozent* at the University of Berlin. Very early in his career he accepted an appointment as Professor of Economics at Freiburg, becoming successor to the great economist Karl Knies. Not long after this he suffered a severe nervous breakdown which required his retirement from academic life. For the greater part of his productive career he lived as a private scholar in Heidelberg. During World War I he accepted an appointment at the University of Vienna, and later—in 1919—he was appointed to the chair of Economics at Munich. During this period he was an active member of the delegation to the League of Nations. He died of pneumonia in 1920 at the height of his scholarly powers.[2]

The full stature of Weber as an original scholar became fully clear with the publication in 1904 of *The Protestant*

Ethic and the Spirit of Capitalism.[3] In an atmosphere largely created by Marxist intellectuals, all spheres of life, including the artistic, were being explained more or less exclusively in terms of economics. Political, religious, social, ethical, and aesthetic concerns were interpreted as extensions of economic interests. *The Protestant Ethic and the Spirit of Capitalism* was a dramatic essay in which Weber corrected the simplism of an exclusively economic interpretation of cultural life. Other areas of life were treated as semiautonomous with effects of their own. The thesis that religion is necessarily or only the opiate of the masses was implicitly rejected. Causal influences were traced from religious experience to economics. Many of the distinctive features of Western capitalism were traced from the central attitudes and characteristic modes of deportment generated in the circles of the Protestant sects.

The essay set off one of the great intellectual debates in modern times. From the days of *The Protestant Ethic* to the collected works in the sociology of religion left unfinished at his death, Weber's work ranges over an amazing compass of the modern social sciences. He made original contributions to such different fields as economics, politics and administration, the sociology of religion, the sociology of law, the sociology of authority, leadership, and knowledge.[4]

Weber developed a rich array of concepts which he applied to every area of social life he brought under review, from the sociology of authority to the sociology of music.[5] At bottom sociology studies social action. When the sociologist examines an institution, a group, a community, or a society, he is only studying ways in which people act toward one another, for all things social reduce

to interhuman behavior.[6] Social behavior is not only interhuman but meaningful as well. If in a crowd waiting in
line before a theatre one person steps on another's toe,
there has been a physical contact of individuals but no
social action. When one offers an apology which the other
accepts, the physical act has initiated a temporary social
act. The meanings present in social action are assumed
to exercise a causal influence upon the course that action
takes. A scientist is interested in regularities in the phenomena he studies. For the social scientist, taking meaningful social actions as his object matter, interest attaches
to the kinds of recurrences they display. Accepting the
usual analysis of action into means and ends, Weber iso-
lates certain fundamental ways in which social actions
may be stabilized: through the rational efficiency of
means to achieve the ends desired; through the establishment of ends as fixed; through acting out of an excess of
emotion; through acting habitually, or if the habit is
socially shared, traditionally.[7] In these various types of
action (rational, evaluative, emotional, and traditional)
the properties of action are determined by the relation of
means to ends. In the first (rational) the action is determined by the complete freedom of the choice of ends
and by the choice of means purely in terms of their efficiency. The actions of a scientist are the very epitome of
rationality. A housewife choosing freely among food
values and shopping where she gets the highest quality
of food values at the lowest price is behaving rationally.
An action is evaluative when he ends toward which it is
directed are assumed to be absolutely valid. Religion presents many examples. One may take salvation to be the
unquestioned ultimate value of human conduct and order
all other aspects of life as means to achieve it. One is act-

ing evaluatively when he takes as absolute some value such as honesty and tells the truth on all occasions regardless of the consequences. An artist might take some ideal of beauty as an absolute end and sacrifice fame, fortune, and perhaps even his family and health to it. An action is affective when it is determined by the presence of strong emotion: actions in rage or terror, grief or despair are typical. An action is traditional when determined by long familiarity and habit: when one votes for one party because his family has always done so. Many hundreds of little actions in everyday life are traditional.

There are three primary ways in which action may be regularized: rationally, evaluatively, and traditionally. Most affective or emotional actions are highly unstable and variable. Most societies spend much time controlling unstable affectively determined actions. Collective emotional behaviors, like those of the actions of mobs, are ordinarily avoided when possible.

Since sociologists are interested in recurrent patterns of conduct, an important economy of thought is represented by a concept which permits reference to the pattern without the need to refer to every single act in which the pattern is displayed. For Weber a social relation consists in the existence of a probability that there will be in some meaningfully understandable sense, a course of social action.[8] A social relation is an arrangement of persons present in any social action. If two persons interact in such a way that A always gives orders and B carries them out, one may say that whenever A and B act a social relation of superiority-subordination holds between A and B. The concept of social relation substitutes for the need to refer to a whole multiplicity of specific actions, concentrating on the common pattern.

A social structure is an organized system of social relations. A state, for example, is an extensive system of social relations between officials and citizens. Such social relations when organized into structures are often very specifically defined such that very definite rights and obligations adhere to any single person. A citizen of the state, for example, may be obligated to pay taxes, to fight in its armies, to refrain from certain kinds of actions defined as treasonable. The president of the state receives a specific salary and has a whole series of definite powers and responsibilities, perhaps even with specified punishments (such as impeachment and loss of office).

The stabilities of social action due to rational, evaluative, and traditional forces also apply to social relations and social structures. A scientific laboratory, for example, may represent a stabilized social structure the relations of which are predominantly of a rational type. A religious sect may be primarily characterized by relations of an evaluative nature. A family may display a fundamental system of traditional patterns.

Social actions are the units of interhuman life also in the collective aesthetic life of man. Here, too, social relations are stabilized and social structures appear. The musical life of men also may be organized into a variety of forms. It is evident that to some degree the musical life of men is susceptible to analysis in terms of the same sociological categories as are other areas of life.

Rational Social Action in Occidental Development and Social Structure

One of the most fundamental theses running through Max Weber's many studies is that an ever-growing preponderance of rational social action runs through the development of the Western world. Ultimately this thesis was applied by Weber to the Occidental arts, particularly its music.

The term "rational" does not have a single meaning in ordinary discourse. It has a range of meanings from "reasonable," "representing good judgment," to "conducted in terms of logical or scientific principles." At times ideas, actions, persons, and even social structures are said to be "rational." Modern psychologists, particularly the Freudians, have familiarized us with the concept of rationalization as the psychological process of giving pseudo-reasons for the real ones in conduct, concealing one's true motives from others and often from oneself. The term "rationalism" has been employed to refer to a kind of philosophic outlook such as that current in the eighteenth century.

In applying the term "rational" to social action, Weber was concerned to isolate one kind of relation between the means and ends of action. A social action is rational when the means utilized in the course of action are chosen because of their efficiency or adequacy to the attainment of the ends in view. We can be most certain of the rationality of the choice of means to ends to the degree to which logical or scientific standards have been established permitting judgments of adequacy or appropriateness. To a lesser extent ordinary experience supplies us with many standards of adequacy. A person who tried to cross a stream by flapping his arms and flying over like a bird would hardly be considered to possess an average knowledge of appropriate or adequate means. Modern science has tremendously expanded our knowledge of relations between things of the world; it has enormously widened the sphere of man's rationality.

The term "rational" does not apply to the ends of action or to the values to which action is addressed. This separates the technical from the ordinary usage. A youth who argues with his parents or teachers may be told that he is irrational or unreasonable when often what is actually meant is that he is taking some unusual stand or making some unconventional demand. Such identifications of "rational" with "conventional" blur its meaning by referring it partly to the ends of action. The "rationalism" of the eighteenth-century philosophers was of this type. The rationalistic philosophers believed that every man has a faculty of reason and men share the same universal set of values. Weber's usage has nothing to do with the ends of action, only with the choice of means in terms of their appropriateness to ends. An act of thought conducted in terms of the rules of logic is rational. An act of inquiry conducted in terms of the norms and criteria of science is also rational, for rationality means precisely the conduct of the thought process in terms of such norms and criteria. The technical conception of rational social action as developed by Max Weber is a direct extension of these meanings.

A social relation is an arrangement present in social action; social structure is a complex, organized pattern of social relations. By simple extension one may describe a social relation or social structure as rational. So far as the actions of a young man and girl in love are determined by the presence of powerful emotion they are, in Weber's terminology, affective. When the stirrings of adolescence send the young boys of America into the trees in the girl's front yard to behave in ways leading sager minds to think that perhaps Darwin had a point, such irrationalities are not atypical of affectively determined actions. By contrast, the same girl's elder sisters may employ every artifice with a deliberately calculated rationality. Thus rational social actions may appear even in areas where the most powerful emotions normally appear, such as erotic spheres.

A social structure is rational to the degree to which the system of social relationships rests on an organization of ends to means in terms of efficiency, adequacy, and appropriateness of means to ends. It has already been observed that rationality may even appear in a courtship. Rational strategies may be observed by the staff officers in war. A business corporation may be rationally organized: computing all actions in terms of their effect in increasing profits; basing hiring and firing policies on judgments of efficiency; calculating all assets and expenditures; continually adjusting behavior to cut costs and increase earnings. Not all groups are equally susceptible to rational organization. A business corporation is ordinarily more rationally organized than a love affair; a scientific laboratory is usually more rationally organized than a family; the experiment conducted by a group of atomic scientists is ordinarily more rationally conducted than a blind date. But while differentially susceptible to rational organization, rational structuring of action may appear anywhere.

It was Weber's view that one of the ground trends in Western civilization is the movement toward rationalization. In every institutional area, in the rise of business, in political parties, in government, in religion, calculation in terms of efficiency and the appropriateness of means to ends tends to be the rule. Old mythologies are exposed, taboos are exploded, magical forms are destroyed, and the colorful and varied forms of old mysteries are clarified in the cold light of scientific day. In Friedrich Schiller's phrase, a "disenchantment of the world" is carried out.

Thought itself tends to find its norm in science, the most rational of all thought forms. The economic historians have familiarized us with the idea that our economics is characterized by the development of rational business enterprise for the pursuit of profit. In political administration the Western world has experienced the most complete growth of bureaucracy, the most rational of all administrative forms. Philosophy and theology are driven on to new forms under its impulse.

This process in Occidental culture of disenchantment or, as it is often called, "progress," to which science belongs as a link and motive force, has, according to Weber, gone beyond merely practical and technical spheres to touch the very problem of the meaning of the world. As time went by Weber found himself increasingly turning to the works of Leo Tolstoi, where, he believed, the problem posed by rationalization reaches a critical intensity. As Tolstoi saw it, for civilized man death itself has no meaning. When the life of civilized man is placed in a scheme of infinite progress according to its immanent meaning, it should never come to an end. While for the peasant, like the patriarchs of old, life and death were linked in an organic cycle such that a sense of the completion of life in death was possible, this sense of completion has vanished for civilized man. The process of disenchantment has extended to the very meaning of life and death.[9]

Rationality in the Arts

Weber did not develop his theories as to the relation between the arts and the rest of life. But there is an unexpressed assumption of a continuity. Western man does not change his nature when he turns to his arts. The same thematic tendencies apparent in other spheres of his life are apparent here.

The drive toward rationality, that is, the submitting of an area of experience to calculable rules, is present here. Only in Western architecture had the pointed arch and cross-arched vault been rationally used as a device for distributing pressure and roofing spaces of all forms. Only here had these been turned into the constructive principle of great monumental buildings and utilized as the foundation of an architectural style.

Only in Western painting does the rational use of lines and perspectives come into central focus manifesting a parallel drive toward rational calculability equivalent to the employment of the Gothic arch in architecture.

Printing was invented in China, but only in the West was the rationalization of literature carried through on the basis of printing. Only here does a literature designed only for print make its appearance.

This drive to reduce artistic creativity to the form of a calculable procedure based on comprehensible principles appears above all in music. Western tone intervals were known and calculated elsewhere. But rational harmonic music, both counterpoint and harmony and the formation of tone materials on the basis of three triads with the harmonic third are peculiar to the West. So too, is a chromatics and an enharmonics interpreted in terms of harmony. Peculiar, too, is the orchestra with its nucleus in the string quartet and organization of ensembles of wind instruments. In the West appears a system of notation making possible the composition of modern musical works in a manner impossible otherwise.[10]

In all these areas the experience of Western man is assumed to display a basic continuity of theme from its practical and technical to its artistic spheres. By itself this is no new idea, for the continuity of art and the rest of social life was widely held throughout the nineteenth century and dramatically formulated by Hegel. Many times the judgment has been expressed that music is the most modern of the arts. Or, again, it has been asserted that music is the most spiritual of the arts. It has also been called the most mystic and most emotional of the arts.

Weber's essay, *The Rational and Social Foundations of Music,* undercuts all such relatively superficial estimates by raising the equivalent questions in more specific form. The issue is not simply left with the rhetorical question, To what extent does the structure of Western music display a rationality paralleling that found in other areas of Occidental social, institutional, and technological life? Rather the concrete investigation is carried out in one feature of Western music after another. One may, for example, ask to what extent has our basic musical scale been reduced to an ordered system of rules? By comparison with the scales developed elsewhere it is possible to determine whether greater rationality has been achieved elsewhere—and, incidentally, to establish what is peculiarly Western in our musical scales. Equivalent types of investigation are possible for many other features of Western music.

The remainder of the present essay is concerned with a quick review of Weber's study. For this purpose, it may be presented in four basic divisions: the examination of harmony in its relation to melody; the study of the scale system of Western music in contrast to others; the review of the kinds of solutions possible to polyvocality and polysonority in musical schemes; and an examination of the role of instruments as vehicles of musical rationalization.

Harmony in Relation to Melody

Harmonic chord music is a great and practically unique achievement of Western man. As an aesthetic adventure into the world of simultaneous sound, harmonic chord music is peculiarly dependent on the rationalization of tone relations and progressions. Only on the basis of an ordered structure of sound intervals could one expect to conjoin tones with the anticipation of regular results. If one wishes to achieve pleasant or interesting effects with some combination of tones, if one wishes to reproduce it and create others like it, one is moved in the direction of formulating a comprehensive system of rules for establishing acceptable tone relationships.

The human ear is capable of an enormous range of sound discriminations. The precondition of aesthetic enjoyment of artistically created sound patterns is the fixing of some fundamental pattern of sounds as an acknowledged instrument for the creation of such patterns. Scales have made their appearance in every known society from the most primitive to the most civilized. But harmonic chord music depending upon the exploration of changing patterns of simultaneously sounded tone combinations is hardly capable of equal development with all scales. Weber believed that the diatonic scale resting upon the sound interval of the octave (1 : 2) represented the scale of maximum effectiveness for this purpose. Its primary structure rested on the interval 1 : 2; through successive divisions of the intervals within the octave, the fifth, fourth, the major and minor thirds, and the whole and half tones were obtained (with the exception of the sixth and seventh). Weber called attention to the fact that harmonic chord music resting on a scale permitting a maximum of ordered relations does not in the diatonic scale have a closed logical system. From the very beginning a nonsymmetric division of sounds is evident. The octave is unequally divided into the fourth and the fifth. Harmonic division of the fourth is omitted and the interval of the seventh is left aside.

When one ascends or descends in rows or circles of octaves, followed by rows of fifths or other intervals, these divisions can never meet on the same note. The fifth fifth approaches the third octave by forty-five cents; the seventh fifth surpasses the fifth octave by fifty-seven cents; the twelfth fifth reaches beyond the seventh octave by only twelve cents. So far everything is in order. All this changes, however, when in accord with harmonic rules one forms the seventh, and the entire logical structure tends to come apart at the seams. A suppressed sense of excitement attaches to Weber's discussion of this problem that transcends any mere passing curiosity over the fact that there is an uneliminatable logical looseness which appears at the heart of harmonic chord music. It cannot be dismissed, apparently, with the question, What's the difference?

There is almost a sense that one has touched one of the ultimate boundaries of human reason itself. In the West a great drama is under way in the extension of man's reason. In one area after another, colorful old mysteries dissipate like morning mist in the cold light of reason and the process of disenchantment of the world is irreversible. One area after another of human experience is transformed into a problem of arithmetic. Who would abandon the formidable gains of the logic and science of Western man? At the same time, in all honesty who would deny that it is more than nostalgic to look with regret at the disappearance of one colorful old mystery after another. We are like children who are told that there is no Santa Claus, nor Easter Bunny, and later no stork. The room for free flight of the imagination is circumscribed by the rules of logic. The spheres to which the attitudes of humility, astonishment, and awe are appropriate vanish. The attitudes around which the psychology of Western man are built are matter-of-factness and unemotional logical perception. The world of Western man belongs not to his heart but to his head. No day goes by without some new area becoming inappropriate to his emotional apprehension as it is clarified in his intellectual perception.

There is, of course, no absolute antithesis between reason and emotion, rationality and irrationality, logic and love. This, however, should not blind one's perception of the fact that they may and, in Western man, repeatedly have come into tension. This may be seen when the most ultimately evocative emotional area of all, Death itself, may be rendered meaningless by the peculiar development of the rationality of Western man.

In Western music the drama of the experience of Western man is re-enacted. Practically his music is addressed to the simultaneous requirements of expression and reason. The history of tuning and temperament, according to Weber, reflects the contradictions betwen theoretical and practical needs. Harmonic chord music does not from the onset rest on a rationally closed system. It is based on triads obtained through intervals which are the result of the first two successive divisions of the octave: the fifth and third. If both intervals are used in ascending and descending fashion, the complete tone material of the diatonic scale, both major and minor, is covered. By obtaining fifths and thirds, up and down, from any given tone, an intervallic discrepancy known as a diesis will result.

Thus, harmonic chord music rests on a rationally divided system of basic tone relationships, but basic to the system is a residual irrational division the consequences of which form a primary object of theoretical reflection for Occidental musical theorists.

The intervals of the diatonic scale have been decided by tonality and harmony. While sounds may be perfect according to the pythagorean theory of acoustical laws, when sounded together they may produce unpleasant effects. The introduction of harmony led to a change in the intervals established by the Greeks. That between the D and E and between G and A were lessened and that between E and F and A and C were increased. The diatonic scale with C as a keynote already had two semitones. The addition of the black keys of the piano or organ suggests a continuous succession of semitones. However, the semitones do not represent a continuous succession of regular tone distances. A given tone like A when counted downward from the tone above A, which is B, is not identical with the first. A-sharp will be a little below the second, B-flat. This difference is a pythagorean comma. The differences of opinion between physicists and musicians have been a central point of theoretical discussion. These problems emerged as harmony became pursued as an objective separate from melody. The tonic and the keynote became the two terminal points within which the attempt was made to fix the intervallic system of the diatonic scale.

In connection with tonality, modulations, inversions,

and cadences become important. Tonality remains undisturbed as long as dissonances can be resolved into consonances, i.e., triads. But precisely the most important dissonance of all, the seventh chord is built on the upper fifth of a tone, the dominant seventh chord. It emerges not as a product of arithmetic division but as an extension of the diatonic scale progression. Another third is added to the triad. But the seventh cannot be included in triadic calculation.

The irrational nature of the seventh chord is emphasized, furthermore, by the fact that whenever its root is omitted, a diminished chord is present; whenever the minor seventh is altered to the major, an augmented chord arises. Diminished and augmented chords form fragments of altered scales which differ considerably from the diatonic scale.

Seventh chords are not derived harmonically, and they cannot be established on purely harmonic grounds. Since they are the result of the transposition of a third, the result of a change of pitch level, they should be accounted for through melodic needs. Harmonic chord music, thus, is not only made up from tone relations which are the result of arithmetic divisions manifest in the organization of the diatonic scale, and its intervals, in triads and their respective tonality; it is also influenced by melodic devices of tone proximity. Harmonic chord music is no mere sequence of triads, of harmonic dissonances and their resolutions, but an exchange between the latter and chords which do not stand for a key, a tonality, a fixed function within a tonality, tones whose melodic function has been explained as "passing, sustained, anticipated tones," and "appogiaturas" or "suspensions."

Harmonic chord music, thus, consists of a fluctuating

tense interpenetration of the harmonic principle by another, that of tone proximity. These chord alien tones are considered by Weber as the most effective means of the dynamics of chord progressions. Without their irrational tensions, no modern music could exist. The irrationality in modern music is given through its melodic-dynamic harmony.

A great many of these nonchord tones have been treated by Hindemith in his *Craft of Musical Composition* as offshoots of chords. What Weber describes as dynamics of chord progression Hindemith describes as follows: "But there are many such tones which do not produce independent chords, chord splinters, or offshoots, they might be called. Such tones enrich chords without essentially changing them." And again: "The rigid chordal structure thus has to give up portions of itself bit by bit to melody, the reaction of which in these scrimmages is comparable to that of an acid upon metal. A tiny bit of a mighty force gnaws and bites at the material under attack, not strongly enough to destroy it, and yet affecting the surface enough by etching scratches and grooves into it, to roughen its smooth finish." [11]

This phase of Weber's essay brings into central focus the relations between the harmonic and melodic elements of nineteenth-century music and locates many of the most interesting features of it in the tension between rational and expressive requirements involved. The protagonists of the aesthetic adventure of Western man are seen as driven to attain a maximum of logical order, rationality, on the one hand, and the intensified, lyric, free, creative expression, affectivity, on the other. This is the aesthetic counterpart of the drama of Western man in other areas of his life.

The question could be proposed: Has Western music achieved the maximum rationality within the limits of expressive possibility? Has one, here, finally located one of the ultimate limits of rationality itself? Could one have simultaneously achieved greater rationality and more full expressive flexibility with some other scale system?

Having posed the problem of harmonic rationality and melodic expressiveness in a characteristic manner, Weber deepens the level of his analysis by raising the question of the limits of the rationality of the Western scale system through comparison with prediatonic and Eastern-Asiatic musical systems.

Prediatonic in Relation to Western Scale Systems

Weber reviewed the literature of his day on Eastern-Asiatic musical systems in connection with the controversial role of the seventh in nineteenth-century European harmonic chord music. In the course of this review Weber came to a number of conclusions: (1) The state of rationalization of the scale system cannot be improved through the utilization of the integral 7 or by still higher prime numbers. This is revealed by numerous examples of scales in the Eastern-Asiatic area resting on the seventh upper partial and the tritone. (2) In contrast to the use of the integral 7 as a basis for rationalization, the musical system of the Greeks and the early Christian church eliminated the number 5 and thereby the diatonic scale, the differentiation between major and minor, tonality and triads. It is an old story that modern harmonic music was only possible by changing all this. (3) In systems such as the Greek and the modal system of the early church, devices playing the role of tonality are of interest. In these systems the harmonic third was supplanted by the ditone, the semitone by the limma. In lieu of the harmonic division of a fifth and a conjunct fourth, the division into two equal fourths each consisting of equal whole tones is introduced. The instrumental division with its tone relationships is replaced by an intervallic division in which modulations, the principle of tone proximity, is of constructive importance.

In the course of this review of the musical systems of the Eastern-Asiatic area, of the Greeks, and of the early church, Weber appears to suggest that a maximum of rationality, within the limits of a range of expressive possibilities, has been achieved in Occidental music. Presumably any further rationality could only be secured by the sacrifice of expressive plasticity.

Weber turned next to the problem of expressiveness bound up with the principle of tone proximity and intervallic distance. This was the motivating interest in his review of prediatonic scale systems. Numerous examples of pentatonicism were reviewed to determine the full nature of the contrast between harmonic and melodic music, between music with and without triads.

Pentatonicism is characterized by the utilization of the frame of two equal tetrachords into which an additional tone is added. The fact that two equal tetrachords are used presupposes the subdivision of the octave. The acceptance of the octave as a basic point of departure shows partial rationalization (in the sense of harmonic chord music).

Since pentatonic music is partly rationalized, as found, for example, in the systems of the Chinese and slendro scales of the Javanese, it must be distinguished from primitive music. The same would hold for the pentatonicism of the Jewish synagogue and of the Roman Catholic Church as well as the music of the Indians, Mongols, Papuans, and Fulah Negroes.

Innumerable studies in comparative and ethnomusicology have confirmed the wide distribution of pentatonicism. Although pentatonicism is to be distinguished from primitive music, it had some things in common with it. Moreover the music of many primitive tribes, such as the ceremonial music of the Chippewa Indians, was of a pentatonic nature. Chromaticism or semitone music, for instance, was used by primitive tribes as well as by representatives of the Eastern-Asiatic cultures. It appears in Negro melodies as well as in Japanese music. The avoidance of the expressive half-tone devices can also be found in the music of many North American tribes and in the musical systems of the Chinese and Cambodians. In both primitive and pentatonic music the major third or its harmonically measured equivalent is extremely rare. However, a great variety of imperfect thirds is to be found.

In both primitive and pentatonic musical culture we often find pentatonic scales in addition to other scale devices. The Hindu Râga system had seventy-two in all.[12]

It is not possible to determine the extent to which the seven-tone or octave scales originated out of alterations and corruptions of pentatonic scales. There is no doubt, however, as to the importance of the pentatonic scale for the history of scale development toward the seven-tone and twelve-tone scales, nor is there any doubt as to the rationalistic organization of a tetrachordal tonality in contrast to authentically primitive scales which consist of unorganized conglomerations of nonrational tone successions.

The complexity of prepentatonic, pentatonic, prediatonic, and diatonic development of scale formations in many primitive societies, a problem, partially, of the reciprocal influence between tonality, scale formation, and society is brilliantly described by Weber in terms of the insertion of auxiliary and filler tones within the rationalized frame organization of the fourth. Driven by melodic requirements such filler tones may range from a quarter-tone to a third. Tetrachordal scales using these melodic forces for the selection of intertetrachord intervals are far more free for scale formation than any harmonically designed scale.

Eastern-Asiatic theorists experimented with a great many scales consisting of such novel intervallic combinations within the diazeutic fourth. Residues of these theoretic scales can be seen in the division of the Greek tetrachords into the chromatic and enharmonic genders, giving the specific role of affective and expressive meaning.

Similar evidences of melodic microtonal formations are present in the seventeen Arabian third tones,[13] the śruti system [14] of Hindu music with its twenty-two equal tone steps to the octave. Survivals from equivalent theoretic scales can be seen in certain local scales of Greek origin which refer to specific filler tones of the corresponding tetrachords (Dorian, Phrygian, Lydian).

It may be noted that in the passages where Weber raises these issues he has touched an important social factor affecting the basic scales and the possibility of their rationalization. Such theoretic systematization and ingenious experimentation with microtonal intervals has often been the work of professional musicians interested in two artistic values: increasing expressiveness on the one hand and codifying procedure on the other.

Another kind of general sociotechnical influence is apparent so far as the requirements of instrumental tuning may affect melodic intervals. If they are to be used together, one instrument has to be tuned to the other. The tuning of wind instruments, for example, may be adapted to that of string instruments, as seems to be the case in the semitone and microtone tetrachord tuning of the aulos and kithara.

A kaleidoscopic picture of the intervals as established within the tetrachords is presented in the tuning of the five-string Arabic lute with its twelve chromatic tones, in pythagorean tuning, and five additional and irrational intervals which increase the number of chromatic tones to seventeen, due to the fact that some intervals were used in an ascending, others in a descending fashion. In general, however, the effect of instrumental tuning is toward the fixing of rational intervals.

Another possible rationalizing influence in the early development of music is language. Linguistic practice sometimes moves in the direction of creating a tone language based on shifting pitch levels and changing tone volumes. Idiomatic melodicism, by producing clear intervals, may have helped in the fixing of rational intervals as well as in the establishment of the musical motive and its repetition. In the latter case, one rationalizing element such as language is substituted for another, i.e., the repetition of a musical motive on a different pitch level makes the equalization of the motivic intervals necessary. The latter can be achieved only through the rationalization of melodic intervals. Thus a chain reaction of rationalization may already occur at the level of pentatonic music.

However, too much must not be made of the relation

between music and language, for it has been proved by Stumpf,[15] Revesz, and others that speech does not know fixed intervals. The movement of speech tones depends exclusively on the prevailing mood of the person at the time of speaking. Nevertheless, an interdetermination of language and music is evident in the range of the melody. In ceremonial formulae of magical or sacred character small intervallic range and stepwise melodic progressions are preferred.

While language and instruments both contribute important rationalizing influences to musical culture, special interest attaches to the effects of the use of instruments in connection with the secular music accompanying dance songs. Curt Sachs proves convincingly that instrumental music, as seen primarily through the history of the drum and flute, derived from magical rationalization.[16]

Secular music and dance forms of instrumental music break through the small, litany-like range of intervals of vocal and sacred music. The range is extended. Tone steps become tone skips. Through instrumental performance, large intervals such as the octave, fifth, and fourth are recognized, established, rationalized, and utilized as consonances. The clear recognizability of these larger intervals permits development of an elementary prediatonic feeling for tonality. Instrumental activities in these secularized contexts have been of paramount importance in the rationalizing of tone intervals.

Magicians, Virtuosi, and the Rationalization of Music

Max Weber's discussion of magicians and virtuosi form a part of his general review of prediatonic scale systems and the music of the immediately premodern period. It has rather special sociological interest since it contains the question of the influence upon musical culture of social roles.

Weber believed that at relatively early cultural levels of human civilization, alongside purely personal, emotional, or aesthetic enjoyment of music there appears music designed for socially important and practical requirements. Music may be present as a magical device designed to serve cultic (apotropaic) or medicinal (exorcistic) ends. Weber maintains that whenever music is used in the service of such magical practices it tends to assume the form of rigidly stereotyped magical formulae. The intervals of such magically effective musical formulae are canonized: classified rigidly into right and wrong, perfect or imperfect. The same applies to the accompanying instruments. Such magical mottoes were identified as highly arbitrary and incomplete scales.

A magical fixing of forms serves rationalization indirectly. For in music as in other areas of life magic may be a powerfully antirational force. But the fixing of intervals serves the purpose of establishing a set of forms against which others are to be tested. In this it may serve as the basis for a uniform musical culture. The people who realized this anonymous rationalization of invocatory formulae were priests and magicians, probably the world's first professional musicians. Unquestionably melodic formulae serving various deities were the source of rationalized scale formations such as the Dorian, Phrygian, and Lydian. Weber attributes to the magician a role in musical development equivalent to that attributed to him by other thinkers in intellectual development.

Special interest attaches to the role of magic in musical development from a sociological point of view for still another reason. Weber, it has been noted, analyzed behavior into rational, evaluative, traditional, and affective types. Magical actions are of an evaluative or traditional type, operating in terms of fixed means and ends and traditional stereotyping. They are thus able to promote rationalization only to a limited degree, for when magical requirements lead to the stereotyped fixing of instrumental use and intervallic pattern, experimentation is discouraged. In extreme cases the slightest deviation from a magico-musical formula is punished by instantaneous death. Moreover, so long as the musical scale is restricted to special occasions for magical reasons, it is withheld from free development.

On the other hand, a professional stratum has been created. It has become the bearer of a uniform musical development. The very magical fixing of musical formula trains both the musician and the audience in the exact perception and rendition of the musical intervals involved.

The reverse situation to the influence upon musical rationalization played by the magical musician is presented by the musical virtuoso. He appears when sacred tones are transplanted into nonreligious contexts and adapted to aesthetic needs. Here experimentation rather than stereotyping may be the rule. Accompaniment by instruments is sought rather than impeded, and it in turn forces an interpenetration of musical and technical requirements. Music addressed to aesthetic and expressive needs may deliberately savor the bizarre. Progressive alteration of intervals in the interest of greater expressiveness may occur, even leading at times to experiment with the most irrational microtones. Purposeful rationalization becomes apparent when tones lying close together are not permitted simultaneous use. This is made possible by the organization of typical tone series such as the Greek, Arabic, Persian, and Hindu scales permitting the tuning of instruments. The full chromatic scale was available on both the aulos and the kithara. The Arabic lute contained all rational and irrational intervals. The dissolving influence of musical virtuosi upon fixed musical structures under the impulse of sheer expressive needs is not confined to premodern stages of musical culture. Weber saw the musical virtuosi as one of the forces eating away the structure of tonality itself.

Early stages of melodic rationalization in the field of sacerdotal music is further exemplified by Weber through three characteristic elements of the later church modes: the concluding formula, the *tonus currens,* and the *tropus.* Illustrations from Vedda music demonstrate the priority of the concluding formula and outline reverse procedure in musical composition. Starting with a fixed concluding formula, musical development may lead to the fixing of the prefinal cadence and, in time, the remainder, and eventually the beginning of the piece.

In Western development musical rationalization appears to have been determined by two factors: the concluding formula and *tonus currens.* Primitive musical systems have fixed rules for concluding formulae. The *tonus currens* forms the melodic center and is usually situated in the middle of the tonal system. It is the *mese* of the Greek greater perfect system, the *finalis* of the plagal church modes, the initial tone for ascending and descending motion, for tuning, transposition, and modulation. The combination of the concluding formula and the *tonus currens* establish melodic tonality. However, when music develops into an art of virtuosi, the predisposition for fixed concluding formulae, cadences, or principle tones is abandoned.

Principal tones within purely melodic musical systems are the so-called "up tones" appearing in descending concluding formulae. Their function should not be confused with that of harmonic leading tones. The final note may consist of the frame tones of the fourth, but in systems which do not possess tetrachordic structure, it may be made up of tones from any other interval. The initial tone may be equivalent to the final tone or related to it as in the case of the church modes. On the other hand, in Greek music the initial tone is not related at all to the final tone.

Throughout this discussion, it may be seen, Weber assigns complementary roles to the magician-musician and virtuosi in the rationalization of music. Under the influence of magic, fixed musical forms are established and a class of priest musicians appears. Under the influence of magic rigid upper limits on rationalization are established. When such formulae are released from magico-religious contexts and when the professional musician is free to employ such musical formulae in secular contexts, actions cease to be evaluative and traditionalistic and may become rationalistic and affective. Often for expressive reasons the virtuoso explores musical effects gained precisely from violation of fixed final formulae and the *tonus currens* of the melodic system.

The frame tones of concluding formulae, most often the fourth and fifth, are, thus, in the course of the histories of their migration from magical-religious to secular contexts, freed by the virtuosi to serve as the basis for rationalizations of the systems in which they occur.

Weber discusses at length the importance of the fourth and fifth for the rationalization of music, their occurrence in modulations both of primitive and art music (Javanese and Ewe Negro). The fourth is a fundamental melodic interval. The fifth arose to importance in instrumental tuning. While in Greek and Byzantine music systems the fourth was predominant, its role fluctuated in the church modes. It became a dissonance in the Middle Ages through applications of the successive divisions of the fifth into the thirds of many-voiced art music.

There were many reasons why the interval of the fourth gained the upper hand over the fifth in ancient music. Weber observes that it is the smallest unambiguously consonance-making interval. It tends to come to be relied upon for rational division in musical systems resting on the principle of intervallic distance. Moreover, in polyphonic singing the higher of two voices tends to monopolize the melody, forcing the lower to adjust melodically to it on the fourth.

Co-operation and competition of both fourths and fifths is illustrated in the unsymmetrical organization of the double octave of the Greek greater perfect system. The two octaves are built upon diazeutic and conjunct tetrachords and an additional lower tone (proslambanomenos) respectively. The lowest tetrachord is in fourth relationship with the next lowest tetrachord, while the latter is in fifth relationship with the next higher tetrachord.

$$A \quad B\rule{1cm}{0.4pt}e\rule{0.5cm}{0.4pt}a \quad b\rule{0.5cm}{0.4pt}e'\rule{0.5cm}{0.4pt}a'$$

The frame tones of the tetrachords were considered immovable and fixed. Modulations could only occur through these frame tones. An additional Bb string was added for modulatory purposes. A new middle tetrachord was obtained which was not in fifth but in fourth relationship. The shift from the fifth to the fourth was considered to be a modulation. Further examples of the combination of disjunct and conjunct tetrachords are found in the octave organization in Arabic and Javanese systems.

Weber's study of prediatonic scale systems and of the problems presented by premodern musical forms is not by any means simply one more history of music. It is a comparative and analytical study of prediatonic musical systems to determine the degree to which they were rationalized, the forces operating for and against rationalization, and the probable directions that rationalization could assume. Only in this way could the full peculiarities of Occidental musical development be established. It would make little sense to characterize Western music as the most rational if more rational models were available than are represented by it. If there actually was a movement within musical development such that steps toward more rational structure tended always to prevail over their opposites, it should be possible to establish the stages by which the rational forms emerge. As one is able to trace the stages in the emergence of more rational thought models, or more rational forms of administration, or business, it should be possible to trace the stages by which the rational elements of premodern music anticipate modern music. It should be possible to clarify the forces bringing this about.

Weber found premodern music to be far less rationalized than our own. When it was rationalized it tended to be on different principles: melodic rather than harmonic. Premodern music with its often baroque multiplication of rational and irrational microtones was often as expressively subtle as it was harmonically crude.

Within this music various factors were operative for and against a harmonic type of rationalization: the magical fixing of musical motives; the rationalizing influences of language and instrumental tuning; the expressive experimentalism by virtuosi in secular contexts. Of very particular importance were those developments which began to occur in early church music with the adaptation of the musical tradition to the requirements of singing choruses. Most of these forces for musical rationalization were present in the music of other cultural areas. But in the West the trend demonstrable in other spheres of life also appears in its music and the more rational forms always tend to prevail.

Polyvocality and Polysonority in Relation to Musical Rationalization

The rationalizing process that emerges and guides the development of Western musical culture reaches a kind of definitive stage with the mastery of problems of polyvoiced music. It forms the point of no return, the point beyond which something quite new appears.

Polyvoiced music is not confined to the Occident. While it appeared also in Oriental cultures, it followed a peculiar course of development in the West. It developed through contrapuntalism to diatonicism.

In Greek, Eastern-Asiatic, and various primitive cultures, polyvoiced music appeared in the form of heterophony, the simultaneous sounding of a given melody and its motivic variation, extension, and improvisation. Weber excludes from his concept of polyvoiced music the many-

voiced singing in unisons or octaves, anticipating the viewpoint of Curt Sachs and other musicologists who main-
tain that parallel octaves are the unavoidable result of
any vocal co-operation of the two sexes and therefore
practised by peoples on the lowest level of civilization.[17]

Three basic types of polyvocality are distinguished: the
modern chordal harmony or "polysonority" (to use
Weber's term) in which the fullness of chordal sound effects is of primary importance; contrapuntal polyphony
in which all participating voices have equal rank, their
progression being submitted to specific rules or prohibitions (heterophony is a preparatory stage of this polyphonic type of co-ordinated music) and harmonic homophonic music, in which the entire tone setting is
subordinated to one voice, it being the melodic vehicle.

Weber reviews the parallels of chordal harmonic and
polysonorous music found in Oriental and Eastern-Asiatic
systems. He maintains that though musicians in these
areas were familiar with the simultaneous sounding of intervals, they did not perceive triads as such, but as combinations of other intervals. In his examination of contrapuntal polyphony, his discussion of such techniques as
canon, fugue, and imitation is followed by the presenta-
tion of rules, the tritone problem, dissonance in contrapuntal polyphony and in chordal harmony, and the prohibition of parallelism. These discussions serve to reveal,
often in fascinating manner, the complexities that sur-
round the stages in the emergence of rational harmonic
forms.

Weber tried both to characterize precisely the three
types of polyvocality and to develop the reasons why they
appear in some parts of the world but not in others. He
explores the bearing of various factors on the local emer-

gence of polyvocal forms: the different tempo adequate for the use of instruments by themselves in contrast to that required when they are used in relation to a vocal part; the significance of the sustained tones of instruments in relation to the plucked ones of the strings; the role played in antiphonal singing of the sustaining of one voice during the entrance of others; the importance of the sonority of the repercussion tones of the harp at the arpeggio; the role of simultaneous chance tone-production while tuning instruments. Any one or any combination of these phenomena could lead to the perception of the aesthetic effects to be achieved through one or another form of polyvocality.

In Western music practically all the conditions that could bring the aesthetic effects of polyvocality to attention were present. If the effects to be achieved through polyvocality are once accepted as a primary musical objective, an extraordinary powerful stimulus for further rationalization is present. The rationalization process plays a considerable role in bringing polyvocality to the fore; polyvocality plays back upon musical development as a tremendous incentive to further rationalization. This spiral of rationalization can give rise to others.

Western musical notation is in considerable measure a product of the movement in Western music toward polyvocality. The acceptance of polyvocality in the monastic chant in the ninth century intensified the need to develop a more adequate musical notation than was offered by the neumes. The first important step, the insertion of the neumes into a system of staff lines appeared as an aid to sight reading of music in singing. The notational improvement of the neumes was secured by transforming them into dots, squares, and oblongs—a product of the requirements of musical pedagogy. Mensural notation of the twelfth century made the establishment of relative time value of tone symbols possible. It became easy to survey the unambiguous determination of relations of progression of individual voices. A true polyvocal composition had become possible.

Notation always retained its character as a compromise between theory and practice, the harmonic and intervallic, the rational and irrational. In the case of the neumes there was no differentiation of whole and semitone steps. This very ambiguity favored the penetration of popular vocal traditions into musical development. The *daseia* notation of the *Musica Enchiriadis,* most emphatically through the *daseia* sign, attempted to establish an order in the arbitrary melodic patterns. Even with the complexly regulated mensural notation, free space was left to the *contrapunta amente* of the descant part. The figured bass part of the baroque era did not put an end to improvised irrationalities. It did not abandon its right of *musica ficta* in order to balance melodic harshness by chromatic tone alterations. The nature of the compromise also becomes apparent in the chord writing of the nineteenth and twentieth centuries. Notation has to ignore the fact that the chord d–f–a according to provenience is either a genuine minor triad or a musically irrational construction.

In the Western world the extent to which melodious alterations should be included in the notation was continuously discussed. Weber calls attention to the fact that several chorales with purely diatonic intonation were known since the fifteenth century and are sung today with a chromatic alteration. One need only mention, for example, the three original monodic versions of *Christ ist erstanden* and the chromatic alterations of its first phrase in the settings of the Schott *Gesangbuch* by Gesius and in the *Christ lag in Todesbanden* variation of Johann Sebastian Bach.

Weber was fully aware of the fact that chromaticism and all irrational intervals are not necessarily the product of a specifically primitive musical development. In fact the *musica ficta* grew precisely within a musical system which already possessed a rationally regulated polyvocality. On the other hand, music systems which once permanently appropriate one irrational interval are particularly inclined to accept further intervals. The diffusion of Arabic music which experiences a twofold enrichment with increasingly irrational intervals, restricted any development toward harmony, diatonicism, and finally, polyvocality.

The most striking general theme running through this phase of Weber's essay is that polyvoiced music soon reaches a point where its further development can only occur in terms of more efficient notation. Notation in turn makes the achievement of quite new polyvoiced musical effects. The problem of musical notation, thus, is lifted to a position in musical development parallel to the invention of writing for literature or of notation for mathematics.

If one considers the differences in literary efficiency made possible by writing resting on an alphabet in contrast to that of a pictographic writing, or the differences in mathematical efficiency made possible by the use of Arabic rather than Roman numbers, one gets some idea of the importance for polyvoiced music of the development of Occidental systems of musical notation. The mutual rationalizing tendencies of polyvocal music and notation supplies one of the dramatic spiral developments in the musical culture of the West.

Instruments and the Rationalization of Nonharmonic Tones through Equalization and Tempering

In the course of his discussion of prediatonic scale formations, Weber had raised a question as to the extent to which premodern music was rationalized. He had also inquired into the factors that had apparently played a role in the partial rationalization of pentatonic systems. He had come to the conclusion that one of the major factors in establishing such rationalization as premodern systems display is found in instruments and their tuning.

One of the unique features of Western music is its unprecedented development of instrumental music. Nowhere else has it been possible to bring to bear the techniques of science to the problem of instrument construction to the same degree. The problems of tuning and temperament are brought to a new quantatively determined level of problems. A spiral of rationalization appears also here comparable to the one between polyvocal music and notation.

When instruments are the vehicle, rationalization may occur in a partly extramusical manner. There are two basic types of tuning: instrumental tuning according to heard tones, fixed tones, and fixed intervals; instrumental tuning which establishes tones and intervals according to purely visual, symmetrical, and ornamental requirements of instrumental construction. This second type of tuning is illustrated by some Central American wind instruments. The tuning of the main instrument of the Chinese orchestra, the shun,[18] was not determined by musical considera-

tions but by aesthetic requirements for mechanical symmetry. Chinese music demonstrates that intervals created
mechanically can be embodied in musical systems, influencing development in a manner making it unavailable
for harmonic and tonal relations.

One type of rationalistic alteration of the tone system
from within is found in distance tempering. Javanese and
Siamese musical systems supply examples of an octave
simply divided into equally large tone distances. Purely
intervallic tempering is designed to permit the transposition of melodies into any pitch without retuning the instrument.

The most important type of rationalistic equalization
from within the tone system is tempering with regard to
the requirements of chordal and harmonic music. In the
West partial tempering existed for the keyboard instruments since the sixteenth century. The range of these instruments was little more than that of the human voice,
the accompaniment of which was one of their functions.
Under such circumstances tempering depended upon the
balance with the four middle fifths of our present piano
(C–e′) and the purity of the interval of the third.

With the extension in range of the piano and organ and
the rise of an independent instrumental music, the division of the octave into twelve equal distances of twelve
equivalent semitones became necessary. The peculiarity
of this modern temperament is found in the fact that the
practical execution of the principle of distance is treated
and is effective on our keyboard instruments as a tempering of tones which are gained harmonically. Besides the
distance-wise measurement of the intervals is found
chordal and harmonic interpretation of the intervals.

The keyboard instruments and the strings have been

central to development of music in the West so far as instruments have played a role. Through these instruments the using social strata, on the one hand, and the technical traditions available for instrument construction, on the other, had a bearing upon the development of musical culture. This may be seen with regard to the violin.

Organizations of instrumentalists played a role in shaping the development of the modern violin. The playing of the crwth [19] was subject to regulations established by the Congress of Bards in 1176. Practice, thus, is fixed by organization requirements which create a common musical culture, on the one hand, and provide a market for standardized instruments on the other. Toward the end of the Middle Ages the building of stringed instruments was influenced by the guild organizations which appeared in the thirteenth century. These provided a fixed market for manufactured instruments, helping establish the types.

The gradual acceptance of the instrumentalist alongside the singer in the *Kapellen* of kings, princes, and communities fixed their social role. When this fixing of social roles occurred, it gave the production of instruments an even more productive economic foundation.

Since the fifteenth century in close connection with humanistic music theorists, the attempt has been made to provide instruments ready to be played in orchestras. The separation of high and low viols was accomplished with the French *ménétriers*. A standardization of instruments and markets goes on continually.

Uninterrupted experimentation in combination with the different traditional practices of the leading orchestras led to the final separation of the violin, viola, and cello. The supremacy of the violin was secured by the persistent experiments of manufacturers of instruments from Brescia and Cremona. The urge for expressive sonorous beauty and elegance of the instrument were the driving forces in Italy for the continuous technical development of the instrument. Once the violin had reached its final form its possibilities far surpassed the musical potential that had been demanded of it. The capacity of the Amati instruments was not fully exploited for decades. The products of the great violin builders rested on skills gradually acquired in empirical experience.

Similar circumstances appeared in the development of the keyboard instruments. Piano virtuosity developed hand in hand with a heavy harpsichord industry which was based in turn on the demands of orchestras and amateurs. Between the combined force of social requirements and the development of technical skills great changes were brought about in the instrument which was typified. The great builder of harpsichords (the Ruckers family in Belgium) created individual instruments commissioned by their consumers (orchestras and patricians). At this stage manifold adaptation to all possible concrete needs of communities and individuals was possible.

The fixing of the piano occurred in the nineteenth century when it became the instrument typical of the culture of the middle-class home. Interesting social factors played a role in this. The piano was not a product of Italian culture, which did not have the indoor character of the Nordic north. The center of gravity of the production and further technical improvement of the piano lay in Saxony, where middle-class home comfort developed for climatic and historical reasons played the critical role.

Summary

Weber's sociology of music rests on his typology of action, though this is not made explicit. Musical culture is analyzed in terms of the rational and nonrational patterns it displays. The peculiarity of Western music was found in the unusual development of rational structures. The intrinsic properties of this musical rationality was explored analytically and comparatively. The social and technical forces that shaped it were examined. The influence of various sorts of technical and rational, evaluative and magical, traditional and affective forces were reviewed.

In the dynamics of Western musical development lie many tensions between rational and affective motives. The value of musical rationalization is the transformation of the process of musical production into a calculable affair operating with known means, effective instruments, and understandable rules. Constantly running counter to this is the drive for expressive flexibility.

One of the fascinating aspects of Weber's discussion is the patience with which he seeks out every irrational residue, every musical element that escapes or seems to escape the rules. It is difficult not to suspect that it is almost with relief that Weber finds that even at the basis of the most fundamental scale formation lack of symmetry appears. There is more than curiosity in the discovery that melodic and harmonic principles appear in tension which is precisely where Western music assumes its most dramatically effective form.

Here, as in other areas of his sociological analysis, Weber touches his moving theme of the disenchantment of the world. As science banishes the colorful mysteries of old magic, as rational thinking converts all things into calculable relations, Weber suspects that the drive was powerfully present at the heart of Western man's musical culture to transform the highest of his musical expressions into an equation in mathematics.

Don Martindale

Johannes Riedel

THE RATIONAL AND SOCIAL

FOUNDATIONS OF MUSIC

Max Weber's essay, "THE RATIONAL AND SOCIAL FOUNDATIONS OF MUSIC," was written according to Marianne Weber, about 1911 and first published by Drei Masken Verlag (Munich, 1921). It was republished as an appendix to *Wirtschaft und Gesellschaft* (Tübingen: J. C. B. Mohr, 1921). It was reprinted in the second edition, of 1924, and in the fourth edition, 1956.

The division of the essay into chapters and subsections is unique to this translation. In view of the remarkable compactness of the essay and the difficulty of the subject matter, we take this procedure to be of self-evident value for greater ease of reading.

1. HARMONY AND MELODY AS FACTORS

IN THE RATIONALIZATION OF MUSIC

Basic Facts of the Harmonic Chord System

ALL rationalized harmonic music rests upon the octave (vibration ratio of 1 : 2) and its division into the fifth (2 : 3) and fourth (3 : 4) and the successive subdivisions in terms of the formula $n/(n + 1)$ for all intervals smaller than the fifth. If one ascends or descends from a tonic in circles first in the octave followed by fifths, fourths, or other successively determined relations, the powers of these divisions can never meet on one and the same tone no matter how long the procedure be continued. The twelfth perfect fifth $(2/3)^{12}$ is larger by the pythagorean comma than the seventh octave equaling $(1/2)^7$. This unalterable state of affairs together with the further fact that the octave is successively divisible only into two unequal intervals, forms the fundamental core of facts for all musical rationalizations. We shall first examine modern music in terms of this foundation.[1]

The tone material of our harmonic chord music is rationalized by dividing the octave arithmetically or har-

monically into fifths and fourths. Then, leaving the fourth
aside, it is divided into the fifth in the major and the minor
third $(4/5 \times 5/6 = 2/3)$, the major third in the major
and the minor whole tone $(8/9 \times 9/10 = 4/5)$, the minor
third in the major whole tone and the major halftone
$(8/9 \times 15/16 = 5/6)$, and the minor whole tone in the
major and the minor halftone $(15/16 \times 24/25 = 9/10)$.

Proceeding from a tone treated as a tonic, chordal harmony builds on its upper and lower fifth. Each fifth divided arithmetically by its two thirds forms a common
triad. When these triads are placed in the order of an
octave, the entire material of the natural diatonic scale,
starting from the corresponding tonic, forms either a major or a minor tone sequence, depending on whether the
major third is ascending or descending.

Between the two diatonic semitone steps of the octave
there are at one time two, at others three whole-tone intervals. In both cases the second is the minor; the others
are major whole-tone steps. If by forming thirds and fifths
ascending and descending from any tone of the scale one
continues to gain new tones within the octave, two chromatic intervals appear between the diatonic intervals of
the octave. Each forms the interval of a minor semitone
step from the upper and lower diatonic tones, both of
which are separated from the other by a remaining enharmonic interval (diesis).

Both kinds of whole tones produce differently sized remaining intervals between the chromatic tones. Moreover,
the diatonic semitone steps deviate from the minor semitone by a different interval still. Thus while the dieses are
formed by the intervals 2, 3, and 5, they represent three
quite different and very complex quantities. The possibility of harmonic separation by successive divisions of

the integers 2, 3, and 5 reaches its one limit at the fourth, which is only successively divisible by the integer 7. Another limit to the possibility of harmonic separation by divisions of the integers 2, 3, and 5 is reached in the large whole tone and the two semitones.

Fully rationalized harmonic chord music based on this tone material maintains the unity of the scalable tone sequence in terms of the principle of tonality. The unity of the scalable tone sequence is achieved through the tonic and the three primary normal triads any major scale has together with a parallel minor scale, the tonic of which is a minor third lower of the same scalable tone material. Moreover, any triad formed on the upper fifth (dominant) or the lower fifth (subdominant octave of the fourth) is tonal, which means that it is a triad built on the tonic of a closely related (major or minor) key sharing the same tone material with the original scale except for one tone each. Correspondingly, the relationships of the keys are further developed in circles of fifths.

By adding another third to a triad, dissonant seventh chords are formed. The most important is the dominant seventh chord built on the dominant of the key with its major seventh as the third which characterizes the key univocally since it appears only in this key and in this composition as a series of thirds made out of scalable tone material. Any chord built of thirds may be inverted (transposing one or more of its tones into another octave) resulting in a new chord of the same tone number and of unchanged harmonic meaning.

Modulation into another key normally starts from the dominant chords. The new key is clearly introduced by the dominant seventh chord or one of its peculiar fragments. Strict chordal harmony comprises only the regular conclusion of a tone form or one of its segments through a chordal sequence (cadence) clearly characterizing the key. Also this is normally achieved through a dominant chord and the tonic or their inversions or, at least, through distinguishable fragments of both.

The intervals contained in harmonic triads or their inversions are (either perfect or imperfect) consonances. All other intervals are dissonances. Dissonance is the basic dynamic element of chordal music, motivating the progression from chord to chord. Seventh chords are the typical and simplest dissonances of pure chord music, demanding resolution into triads. In order to relax its inherent tension, the dissonant chord demands resolution into a new chord representing the harmonic base in consonant form.

Irrational Properties of the Dominant Seventh Chord

So far, at least, everything appears to be in order. At least with respect to these (artificially simplified) basic elements, the harmonic chord system appears to be a rationally closed unit. However, this is only apparently true. To be representative of its key, the dominant seventh chord should, through its third or the seventh of the key, form a major seventh. However, in the minor scale the minor seventh must be chromatically raised in contradiction to what is required by the triad. Otherwise the dominant seventh chord of a-minor would at the same time be the seventh chord of e-minor. This contradiction is not simply melodically produced, as noted by Helmholtz,[2] for only the semitone step below the octave of the tonic has that independent thrust toward the octave which qualifies it as a leading tone. The contradiction is already contained in the harmonic function of the dominant seventh chord itself when applied to the minor scales.[3] Through alteration from the minor to the major seventh the dissonant augmented triad arises from the minor third out of the fifth and to the major seventh of the minor key. It consists of two major thirds in contrast to the harmonic combination of thirds.

Any dominant seventh chord contains the dissonant diminished triad, starting from the third and forming the major seventh. Both of these kinds of triads are real revolutionaries when compared with the harmonically divided fifths. Not since J. S. Bach could chordal harmony legitimate them with respect to the facts of music. If in a seventh chord, containing the minor seventh, two major thirds are added, the dissonant diminished triad is left as a remainder. If one forms a minor and a major third from it, the seventh is diminished. In this manner the altered seventh chords and their inversions are created. Furthermore by combining scalable (normal) thirds with diminished thirds, altered triads and their inversions are formed.

The tone materials cast up by this type of chord can be formed into the much disputed altered scales. These altered scales and chord categories are harmonic dissonances the resolutions of which may be construed in terms of the rules of a (correspondingly expanded) chordal music. These tone materials can also be applied to the formation of cadences. Characteristically they first made their historical appearance in the minor keys, only gradually being rationalized by musical theory.

All these altered chords are eventually traceable back to the role of the seventh in the tone system. The seventh is also the stumbling block in the attempt to harmonize the simple major scale by a series of common triads. The connecting tone from the sixth to the seventh step demanded by stepwise progression is missing. Indeed, it is only at this place that the steps lack the dominance relationship to each other: the degree of next relationship mediated by the dominants and utilized for the harmonization of triads.

Melodic Determination of Chord Progressions

The continuity of progression in the relation of chords to each other cannot be established on purely harmonic grounds. It is melodic in character. Although harmonically conditioned and bound, melody, especially in chordal music, is not reducible to harmonic terms. Indeed, Rameau's theory [4] that the fundamental bass, i.e., the harmonic root of chords, may only progress in the intervals of the triad, pure fifths and thirds, has also subjugated the melody to rational chordal harmony.

It is also known that Helmholtz in theoretically superb fashion carried through the principle of stepwise progression to the next related tones (according to the overtones of the combination tones) precisely as the principle of pure monodic melody.[5] But Helmholtz was forced to introduce a further principle, the proximity of the pitch of tones. He then tried to fit them into the strict harmonic system partly in terms of the investigations of Basevis [6] partly by limiting these tones, which are explainable only melodically, to a mere facilitating function.

Yet tone relatedness and tone proximity are in irreconcilable contradiction, for the interval of a second, especially the intensive leading semitone step, connects the two tones which are distant in physical relationship. This is aside from the general consideration that the scale of upper partials does not form the perfect basis of a scale. With pronounced imperfection it skips over certain tone steps.

The melodies even of the purest counterpoint are neither broken chords only, i.e., chords projected into the succession of tones, nor are they always coupled in their progressions by harmonic overtones of the fundamental bass. Besides, music could never have consisted entirely or alone of mere columns of thirds, harmonic dissonances, and their resolution. The numerous chords do not grow out of the complications of chainlike progressions alone. They also, and preferably, grow out of melodic needs.

Melody can be understood only in terms of intervallic distance and tone proximity. Chord progressions do not rest upon an architecture of thirds. They are not harmonic representatives of a key and not consequently nor synonymously reversible. Nor do they find fulfillment through resolution into an entirely new chord, but in a chord which characterizes and supplements the key. They are melodic, or seen from the standpoint of chordal harmony, accidental dissonances.

Chord aesthetics is concerned with the harmonically or scale-alien tones of such chords even in the form of passing, sustained, or repeated tones in addition to chordally progressing voices whose varying relations to them impart the peculiar personality of the whole. Again they are treated as anticipations or appoggiaturas of tones which belong to chords coming before or after the strictly harmonic materials. Finally they are treated as suspensions, chord tones foreign to the chords which, so to speak, have pushed tones from their proper place. Thus they do not appear freely like legitimate harmonic dissonances but must always be anticipated. They do not demand the special chordal resolution of harmony. Resolution is primarily carried out by early restoration to the displaced tones and intervals of their rights which were infringed upon by the rebels. Precisely through the contact with chordal requirements these chord-alien tones are naturally the most effective means of the dynamics of progression. At the same time they most effectively slur and entangle chord successions.

Without the tensions motivated by the irrationality of melody, no modern music could exist.[7] They are among its most effective means of expression. The manner in which such expressiveness is achieved falls outside this discussion. Here it should be remembered only as demonstrating an elemental fact of music, that chordal rationalization lives only in continuous tension with melodicism which it can never completely devour. Chordal rationalization also conceals in itself an irrationality due to the unsymmetrical position of the seventh, unsymmetrical in terms of distance. This has its most direct expression in the aforementioned inevitable harmonic ambiguity of the structure of the minor scale.

2. PREDIATONIC AND WESTERN SCALE

SYSTEMS AS FOUNDATIONS FOR

MUSICAL RATIONALIZATION

The C-Major Scale

EVEN physically the chordal harmonic tone system is unsymmetrical. The foundation of its modern structure is the C-major scale. In pure tuning it contains ascending or descending from the seven tones of any octave, five perfect fifths and as many fourths, three major and two minor thirds, three minor and two major sixths, and two major sevenths. Moreover, because of the difference in the whole-tone steps, it contains two kinds of small sevenths (three to 9/6 and two to 5/9) differing from each other by the syntonic comma (80/81). Furthermore the chordal harmonic tone system contains within the diatonic tones an ascending fifth and a minor third, a descending fourth and a major sixth, which when compared with two perfect intervals differ by the same comma and result in the same relationship for the fifth d–a (27/40). Considering the sensitiveness of the fifth to all deviations, this is quite imperfect.

Indeed, the minor third d–f is inevitably determined

by the integrals 2 and 3 (pythagorically determined minor third). This failure of rationalization can in no way be eliminated. D and f are limiting tones of the harmonic C-major scale. This is due to the fact that perfect thirds can only be constructed by means of the prime number 5. Hence, the circle of fifths cannot lead back to the perfect third. This can be interpreted with M. Hauptmann as the unresolvable opposition of the thirds and fifths.[1]

Rationalization in Terms of Integral 7 or Higher Prime Numbers

Evidently rationalization cannot be improved by the employment of the integral 7 or higher prime numbers for the construction of intervals. Such intervals are known to be contained in the upper partials starting with the seventh tone. Furthermore, a harmonic division of the fourth (in contrast to the fifth of our tonal system) is possible only in terms of the integral 7 ($6/7 \times 7/8 = 3/4$).

The natural seventh, the seventh upper partial ($= 4/7$, Kirnberger's "i"[2]) is easily produced with string instruments when the strings are damped softly. It is also produced naturally on all primitive horns. It is believed to be found on Japanese tuning pipes and forms a consonance with c–e–g.

Fasch, therefore, tried to introduce this tone into practical music. So, too, the interval 5 : 7 (natural tritone, augmented fourth, the only interval in perfect tuning on the Japanese pipa lute) may operate as a consonance. Furthermore, all other intervals of 7 such as the Eastern-Asiatic (7/8) intervals as whole tone on the ch'in, the main instrument of the Chinese orchestra, on the lowest octave, and as found in Arabic music and the music of antiquity, may certainly have been known to Hellenistic theorists until the Byzantine and Islamitic periods. They were most certainly known to the Persians and Arabs. However, they may not have been employed in musical practice. Hellenistic theorists even identified such intervals with higher prime numbers. However, in no case has a rational harmonic system been established by means of them which is useful for chordal harmonic music.

It is probable that the developments in Eastern-Asiatic music leading to the theoretical exploration of the integral 7 and higher prime numbers was a product of rationalization undertaken on extramusical grounds. This type of rationalization will be explored later.

It may be noted, however, that the seventh is quite legitimate in musical systems with a basic interval of a fourth rather than the fifth or third. On our piano, designed for chordal music, the seventh upper partial is nullified by the pedal. In string instruments it is nullified by bowing techniques. By contrast in primitive horns it had been driven into the harmonic seventh.[3]

Finally intervals with 11 and 13 are contained in the overtone scale. Chladni claims to have heard them in Swabian folk music.[4] But so far as is known they have not been employed in rationalized musical art any more than the interval of 17 by the Persians in the Arabic scale.

Rationalizations in Terms of the Numbers 2 and 3

Finally, there is a kind of music which eliminates the integral 5 as a basis for intervallic rationalization; thereby the differences in the whole-tone steps are eliminated. This music is limited in the forming of intervals to the numbers 2 and 3 and employs the only whole tone, the

major one (with the relation 8/9), or the *tonus* as the
basis of the interval between the fifth and fourth (2/3 :
3/4 = 8/9). Calculating from below, this music gains six
perfect fifths and as many fourths (from all tones with the
exception of the fourth and the seventh) in the diatonic
octave.

This music secures an important advantage for pure
melodic purposes, the possibility of optimal transposition
of melodic movements in the fifth and fourth. This circumstance largely accounts for the early preponderance
of both intervals. However, such music completely eliminates the harmonic thirds which can only be built in
perfect form by a harmonic division of the fifth, using the
number 5. Thus, the triads, the distinction between major
and minor scales, and the tonal anchorage of harmonic
music in the tonic have been eliminated. Such was the
case in Hellenic music and the church tones of the Middle Ages.

The place of the major third was taken by the ditonus
(e : c = 8/9 × 8/9) and the place of the diatonic semitone by the limma (the remaining interval of the ditonus
as contrasted to the fourth = 243/256). The seventh then
equals 128/243. The harmonic method of gaining tones
was thus brought to an end with the first division of the
octave which was regarded as being divided by the fifth
and fourth into two symmetrical fourth tone sequences
(c–f, g–c) divided by the tonus (diazeutic) in contrast
to both by c through the synaphea, which is the identity
of the final tone of the one connected with the initial
tone of the other (synemmenon).

In such tonal series single tones cannot be thought of as
produced by a harmonic division of fifths, but by a division within the fourth, the latter being the smaller of the

two intervals. Moreover, this is not by harmonic division (which is only possible by means of the seventh) but in terms of the equality of (whole-tone) steps, intervallic distance. The unsimilarity of two whole tones which came into being through harmonic division and the two harmonic semitones had to be omitted. Although made up of 2 and 3 the limma, the intervallic difference between the ditone and the fourth, formed irrational relationships in this pythagorean tuning.

Similar results occur with any other attempt to divide the fourth into three intervallic distances as has been done several times in theory (and perhaps practically in Oriental-Arabian music) but which cannot be done without the use of much higher prime numbers and cannot be employed harmonically.

Pentatonicism

Many primitively rationalized scales content themselves with the addition of only one tonal distance. This is regularly one whole tone within the diazeutic fourth. It is the essence of pentatonic scaling.

At the present time pentatonicism is still the basis of the official Chinese musical system. It was the basis for at least one, probably at one time both, Javanese scales. Pentatonicism can be found not only in Lithuania, Scotland, and Wales, but among the Indians, Mongols, Amanites, Cambodians, Japanese, Papuans, and Fulah Negroes.[5] Many doubtless old melodies of Westphalian songs for children show distinct pentatonic structures such as the anhemitonic structure with no semitones.[6] And the general prescription for the creation of compositions of popular character, to use only the five black keys of the piano—

which form a pentatonic system with no semitones—belongs here. Old Gallic and Scottish music testifies to the sovereignty of the anhemitonic.

In different ways Riemann and O. Fleischer believed that they proved traces of pentatonicism in old church music.[7] Particularly the music of the Cistercians with its puritanical avoidance of aesthetic refinements in accordance with the rules of their order, seems to have been of a pentatonic nature. Moreover, among the scales of the Jewish synagogue, besides hymns which have been built on a Hellenistic-Oriental basis, there is one single pentatonic scale.[8]

Pentatonicism and the Problem of the Semitone

Pentatonicism is frequently closely linked in a musical ethos to avoidance of the semitone step. It has been reasoned that this very avoidance constitutes its musical motive. Chromaticism was an antipathetical principle not only to the old church musicians but to the old tragic poets of the Hellenes. It was even antipathetical to the rational and, as it were, bourgeois musical culture of the Confucians.

In their endeavor for passionate expression, the feudally organized Japanese alone among Asiatic people were strongly devoted to chromaticism.[9] However, the Chinese, Amanites, Cambodians, and Javanese (namely in the slendro scales) show uniform aversion to chromaticism and to all minor chords.[10] It is by no means certain that pentatonic scales are everywhere older than other types. Not unusually they appear beside richer scale types.

The numerous incomplete scales of the Hindus appearing alongside complete octave series only resemble the usual pentatonicism to a small degree.[11] The extent to which they originated out of alterations and corruptions of pentatonic scales is not ascertainable. In most cases the greater age of pentatonic scales, at least when compared to present scales, seems probable.

In the music of the Chippewa Indians (according to the phonograms of Densmore) pentatonicism can be found. This is particularly the case for ceremonial hymns which naturally were preserved in their purest form.[12]

The extent to which adherence to pentatonicism with its rejection of semitones is due to musical superstition even in art music remains uncertain. In China rationalistic grounds supplied the basis for an antipathy to the semitone. On the other hand, genuinely primitive music, i.e., nontonal or little rationalized music, has not been proved to avoid the semitone. The phonograms of Negro melodies show the contrary. Thus it has recently been directly disputed that the original reason for pentatonicism can be found in the endeavor to avoid the semitone step, a position taken, for example, by Helmholtz.[13]

Helmholtz assumed simply that in primitive music an early interruption occurs to the tone series related to the keynote in the next grades. However, the analysis of primitive music shows this to be untenable. Nevertheless, pentatonicism is often found with such a motive (the scale c, d-flat, f, g, a-flat, c as against the c, d, f, g, a, c of the Chinese). The later Javanese pelog scale contains seven steps but the workaday scale has five. In the Japanese scale within the fourth a semitone interval stands next to an empty third.[14] Yet when contrasted to the anhemitonic this can only be found in a minority of cases, as, for instance, in the pentatonicism of the North American Indians.

Utilization of the Third in Primitive Music

At times pentatonicism involves the use of the three intervals, the fifth, fourth, and major third beside which only the semitone remains. If the third is understood to be a harmonic rather than a diatonic distance it could have been produced step by step. In this case the exclusion of the whole-tone step would have been of secondary importance.

Indeed, an interval corresponding to the minor third is naturally involved in pentatonic music so far as it uses the harmonic whole tone (27/32) as well as in pure tuning between d and f in consequence of omitting the semitone (as also occurs in the music of the North American Indians). However, pentatonicism does not encompass the major third or, at least, its harmonic measurement. The major third is rare in genuinely primitive music. However, the interval of the third appears in a great many phonographically recorded musical compositions in impure form, neither as a harmonic third nor as a ditone. This could be a product of strong requirements for tone purity and avoidance of precisely those vibrations characteristic of the third. Or it could be correlated with the increasing unintelligibility of the vibrations. The interval of the third appears as the so-called neutral third which Helmholtz maintains is more or less of a consonance even when produced by stopped organ pipes.[15] It appears so imprecisely as to make improbable the utilization of the pure major third in any relatively primitive scale.

It is hardly probable that the pentatonic scale is actually primitive. As far as anywhere known even in the most primitive music, an interval lying close to the harmonic whole tone is the basis of practical music. However, when the fifth and fourth appear, the interval between them tends to become the foundation of musical practice. Pentatonicism presupposes the octave and divisions as various as possible. Thus it always represents a partial rationalization and cannot be really primitive.

The Fourth as the Basis of Pentatonicism

The structure of the pentatonic anhemitonic system assumes the fourth as the basic interval. The Irish scale which the Synod of Cloveshoe in 747 contrasted to the Gregorian choral as the "way of singing of our Irish ancestors," was used in a chordal fashion in the eleventh century and was free of any semitones.[16] In general when reading an anhemitonic scale f, g, a, c, d, f instead of c, d, f, g, a, c, it contains a second, minor third (pythagorean tone and a half), major third (or ditone), fifth, and sixth. This scale does not contain the third and the seventh, but the fourth and the seventh are missing. In this respect the meaning of pentatonicism is not univocal. Many pentatonic melodies, for example, Scotch melodies and the temple hymn cited by Helmholtz,[17] would correspond to the second type, if we take our concept of tonality as a starting point.

Contrary to the rule, in some areas of the world beginners find it more difficult to sing the fourth, alongside the unsingable seventh, than the third. According to Densmore[18] this is the case for the North American Indians. According to F. Hand, it is also true for the children in Switzerland and Tyrol. This last example, however, could be a consequence of the peculiar evolution of the third characteristic of the North of Europe. This will be discussed later.

The anhemitonicism of the Cistercians paralleled a typical preference for the third. In terms of the facts just reviewed, it is questionable whether the more favorable treatment of the third in North European music mentioned by Helmholtz, which sounds purer because of the large quantity of vibrations from the higher pitches, is due to the participation of women in choir singing from which they were excluded in antiquity. Women were excluded from the choirs of the great cultural centers (Athens, Rome) as well as from the post-antique, ascetically minded, medieval church.

As far as I can see, in the music of native peoples the participation of women in song, appearing in a great many variations, finds its expression in the corresponding distinctness of the expression of the third. However, it must be noted, indeed, that no single opinion establishes the third as the only diatonic interval heard.[19] In the musical theory of the Middle Ages the fourth, parallel with the advancing third, fell among the dissonances (primarily without regard to the organum, etc., because it was not theoretically tolerated either in triads, that is clefs, or in parallel motions, and, thus, it was neglected harmonically as compared to the third). Among the North American Indians, whose pentatonicism is becoming extinct, thirds (minor and neutral ones) also play a significant role.[20]

The intervals of the fifth and the third, though close neighbors, seem historically to have stood in a kind of antagonism which Helmholtz tried theoretically to explain.[21] He assumed that the nature of this antagonism was such that pentatonicism was able to operate with one interval or the other. However, because of the general position of the fourth in ancient music, this is not probable.

As far as our knowledge extends today wherever the octave has been distinguished the fifth and fourth seem to have appeared as the first unique and harmonically perfect intervals. This seems to be the case in the overwhelming majority of all musical systems known to us. Even in those which like the Chinese have not advanced a proper tetrachord theory, the fourth possessed the significance of a fundamental melodic interval. Westphalian children's songs typically ascend and descend by a fourth from the most central tone (g), the melodic tonic.

Both Javanese scales form an octave by means of approximate diazeutic intervals of fourths. One (slendro) has an approximately perfect fourth and fifth with one tone in the center of each. The other (pelog) also ascends and descends from the middle tone by an approximately perfect and sustained fourth.[22] Its customary scale, counting from the lowest tone, contains an initial tone, neutral third, fourth, neutral sixth, and minor seventh. J. C. N. Land thinks the first scale to be of old Chinese, the second of Arabic origin.

Everything considered, pentatonicism should most probably be interpreted as a combination of two diazeutic fourths. If both fourths were originally divided by one interval, each was movable and eventually irrational in terms of melodic motion (particularly if ascending or descending). The Javanese pelog system could be explained in this manner. The clearly authentic proof of a similar evolution, such that first bordering tones of fourths as fundaments of all intervallic semitones became fixed, is to be found with the Hellenes. Proof is also provided by the Arabs and Persians. From here a tone system could evolve which was irrational with exception of the fourth. Development could lead from here to anhemitonicism and

finally to pentatonicism with semitones and the major
third or, like many Scotch songs, also with the whole tone
and minor third. According to Plutarch, the ancient trope
spondee (τρόπος σπονδειάζων) serving as the song of sacrifice for the Hellenes was pentatonic and apparently
anhemitonic.[23] However, the hymn of the second Delphic
Apollo visibily composed in anachronistic style seems to
avoid utilization of more than three tones of a tetrachord,
but not the semitone step.[24] By all odds the older and
most widely diffused meaning of pentatonicism is the
avoidance of semitones or the reduction of them to a
supplementary role as intervals which lead only melodically. Pentatonicism itself already represents a kind of
selection of rational and harmonic intervals from the
abundance of melodic intervals.

Scale Formation on the Basis of Melodic Intervals

In reviewing these phenomena we have left the topic
of the production of harmonic intervals which involve
divisions of the fifth. We have been brought to the problem of scale formation consisting of selection of melodic
intervals within the fourth. This type of scale formation
allows far more arbitrary freedom than any scale designed harmonically.

The scales of purely melodic music have made ample
use of their freedom. This is particularly apparent in musical theory. Once the fourth is taken as the basic melodic
interval, innumerable possibilities, principally arbitrary,
appear for more or less rational division and combination
of intervals. The scales of Hellenistic, Byzantine, Arabic,
and Indian theorists, who apparently influenced one another, show such combinations.

Today it cannot any longer be proved that many of the bizarre scale formations were actually used in fact. The only circumstance suggesting that they were was the presence of an ethos favorable to them. At least in the circles which supported art music the effects of these baroque scales must have been enjoyed. There are indications of this in Oriental theory which influenced Byzantine theory, where they were more frequent and typical than in Hellenistic theory. Information as to musical practice is not altogether reliable.

We are in a better position to judge some practical realities. The question as to the range of musical practice can be partly solved in terms of the pantheon of local tunings of instruments and the adaptation of the tunings of some instruments to others. For example the upper partials (diatonics) of wind instruments may be adapted to string instruments. When this occurs both have become objects of systematic rationalization. Or again, a differentiation of melodic scales, originally local, is manifest in the regional significance of the Hellenistic keys (Dorian, Phrygian, etc.). Similar evidences appear in Hindustan scales and the Arabic division of the fourth.

Some phenomena in Hellenistic and Arabic music suggest an evolution starting with the acceptance of intervals derived from diversified instruments. Alongside diatonic division achieved through pythagorean intervals, the fourth, as known in the Hellenic tone system of classical times, was also divided. The division of the Hellenic fourth was first into a minor third and two semitones (chromatic) and second into a major third and two quarter tones (enharmonic). Finally, both formations were characterized by exclusion of the whole tone. In both cases it is probable that the insertion of thirds left minor tone steps as a residue. It was precisely these tone steps that led to the first harmonically correct calculations: of the major third by Archytas and of the minor third by Erastesthenes.[25] It appears that one inverted to the pyknon, chromaticism and enharmonicism were used as a means of melodic expression. The partly preserved stasimon from *Orestes* by Euripides containing the enharmonic pykna, belongs in dochmic verses to the passionately moving strophes of the piece.[26] Plato's ironical remarks in *Politeia*, the more benign observations of Plutarch, and the discussions of late writers of the Byzantine period prove that the problem of enharmonicism was one of melodic refinement.

With the traditional fixing of the organization of the octave into seven steps (also maintained to be sacred), theory retained only one augmented tone step in the fourth. The chromatic and enharmonic scales most probably first appeared in musical practice with the aulos. The instrument produced irrational deviations from the rational intervals, which were still enumerated by Aristophanes. This supposition in agreement with tradition is further supported by the discovery of an instrument in Bosnia.[27] It is similar to the aulos, producing the chromatic scale of the Hellenes. This is also supposed to be true for Balearic instruments. As with the aulos, chromatic tone production and the correction of irrational intervals was achieved by partly covering the holes. This is similar to old music for the flute. The production of random slur tones and partial intervals is almost inevitable under such circumstances. When such intervals were imposed on the kithara the attempt was made to rationalize them. Controversy increasingly centers on quarter- and third-tone intervals.

However this may be, the intervallic system that appears is far from primitive; it belongs to Hellenic art music. According to papyrus findings, it was unknown to the Aiteles and similar tribes without higher culture. Moreover, traditional chromaticism is thought to be younger than diatonicism and quarter-tone enharmonicism to be still more so. Chromaticism belongs to the classical and post-classical periods. It was rejected by both older writers of tragedies. On the other hand, it was in a state of decay at the time of Plutarch (to his regret). The series of chromatic and enharmonic tones have no tonal relation to our harmonically conditioned concept of chromaticism. Although chromatic tone alterations and their harmonic legitimatization in the Occident historically rest on the same requirements as the pykna of the Hellenes, they are twice transformed. First chromatic tone alterations are transformed by the demand for melodic softening of the severity of the pure diatonicism of the church modes. Later, in the sixteenth century when the majority of our chromatic tones were legitimatized, they were transformed by the demand for dramatic effects.

The same expressive requirements led to a disintegration of ancient tonality despite the theory of the Renaissance which interpreted chromaticism and sought to resurrect ancient tone genders. The same process led on to the creation of modern tonality, founded in the very decaying structure of that music in which these tone formations were embedded. During the Renaissance new chromatic split tones were harmonically formed through third and fifth derivations. Hellenic split tones by contrast, are products of pure intervallic tone formation, originating in melodic interests. The quarter-tone intervals of Hellenic musical practice in late antiquity (according to the re-

marks of Bryennies concerning the *Analysis Organica*)
seem to belong to the string instruments. They still appear in the Orient, be it essentially (or originally) as slur
tones.

Beside these much discussed Hellenic quarter tones, the
Arabic third tones, seventeen for each octave, have played
a prominent and easily misunderstood role in musical history since the works of Villoteau and Kiesewetter.[28] Following the more recent analysis of Arabic musical theory
by Collangettes, the seventeen-tone octave probably originated as follows.[29] Before the tenth century the scale
seems to have consisted of nine tones in the octave (including the initial tone of the octave, ten): for instance,
c, d, e-flat, e, f, a-flat, a, b, c. These were interpreted
as two fourths conjoined through the tone f beside which
is found a diazeutic tone step (b–c). Since this octave
depended exclusively on pythagorean tuning,[30] it almost
certainly derives from Hellenic influence. However, the
fourth, in addition to being divided by a tone and ditone
from below, is also divided by a tone from above. The
old Arabic instruments, particularly those deriving from
the bagpipe, the instrument proper to all nomads, have
supposedly never accommodated themselves to this scale.
Thus, there was a strong tendency to extend toward the
pythagorean third and beyond this to an additional third.

Influence of Musical Reformers and Instruments on Scale Formation

In the growth of the Arabic scale the rationalism of
the music reformers was felt. They unremittingly and in
most varied forms applied mathematical theory to balance
the tuning caused by the asymmetry of the octave. Later

we shall discuss the products of this enterprise. Here we are only tangentially concerned with them.

In Arabia the bearer of the extensive and intensive evolution of the scale was the lute (the word is Arabic). In the Arabic Middle Ages it became the instrument decisive for the fixing of the scale intervals. This parallels the function of the kithara for the Hellenic world, the monochord for the Occident, the bamboo flute for China.

Traditionally the lute had first four, later five strings. Each was tuned a fourth higher than the lower one; each comprised a fourth; each was characterized by pythagorean tuning, the whole tones of the fourth being divided into three rationally obtained intermediate tones. These were whole tones from above and ditones from below (thus c, d, e-flat, e, f in pythagorean definition).

It must be assumed that some of these intervals were used in an ascending fashion, others in a descending manner. When theoretical considerations led to the ordering of all tones in the same octave, the result was twelve chromatic tones, defined pythagorically. However, the central interval (e-flat) was irrational defined differently by the Persians and the music reformer Zalzal.[31] Then, since one of these irrational intervals in conflict with the other maintained itself on the lute next to the diatonic interval, this meant that in each of the five others there existed one interval or more which ordered within the octave involved an increase of chromatic tones from twelve to seventeen.

Between the tenth and thirteenth centuries, in the practical division of the lute, the pythagorean and both kinds of irrational intervals were used in a miscellaneous fashion. They were arranged within the octave scale in such manner that both irrational thirds were accepted between e, e-flat–e, and a-flat–a. However, between c–d and f–g, as we would say in their function as leading tones to the lower whole tone, a pythagorean limma (ditone as counted from the upper whole tones f or b respectively) originated. Moreover, one semitone distance was obtained through quite irrational intervals, each of which corresponded to one or both irrational thirds. Thus, altogether three intervals were included such that within the fourth c–f the scale originated: c, pythagorean c-sharp, Persian c-sharp, Zalzal's c-sharp, pythagorean e-flat, Persian e, Zalzal's e, pythagorean e, f. In the same manner the fourth f–b was divided. Obviously only one of the three categories of intervals could be present in one melody.

In the thirteenth century the Arabic scale was brought to fractions and powers of the numbers 2 and 3 and defined through the circle of fifths. As a result both fourths contained the second and the ditones from above and from below (the upper fourth moreover, contained the second from below) and, in addition, two tones each being separated from the other by the interval of a second, the lower of which was separated from the lower whole tone by two limmata so that the upper was separated from the upper whole tone by the interval of the apotome (equals a whole tone minus the limma) minus the limma. For example, this had a result as follows: pythagorean g-flat, pythagorean g-flat plus limma g, pythagorean a-flat, pythagorean a-flat plus limma a, pythagorean a, b.

Finally, modern Syrian-Arabic calculation (M. Meschaka) [32] distinguishes twenty-four quarter tones in the octave, and emphasizing the most important intervals in music, divides both conjunct fourths by a whole-tone step (8/9) equating the latter with four quarter-tone and two different three-quarter–tone steps: 11/12 and 81/88, both equaling three quarter tones. These seven intervals most frequently applied in practice could, thus, represent the second, the old Zalzal sixth (equals a fourth above the Zalzal third), the minor seventh as the final tone of the upper fourth so that from there the diazeutic whole-tone step might remain to the upper octave. In all these cases of quarter or third tones the significant point is that these are intervals, to be sure not of harmonic origin, but they are really not equally large. This is true as we shall see later in the case of tempered intervals though musical theory is inclined to regard them as a kind of intervallic common denominator of so-to-speak just audible musical atoms. Plato scoffed at this notion. The same is valid for the śruti calculation of Hindustan art music with its supposedly twenty-two equal tone steps for the octave, while the major whole tone is set equal to 4, the minor equals 3, the semitone equals 2 śruti.[33] Such microintervals are a product of the immeasurable abundance of melodic distances differing from one another as a result of local differentiation of the scales.

The Chinese division of the octave into twelve lü,[34] which theory conceived as equal but which are not practically treated in such manner, illustrates the inexact theoretic interpretation of the diatonic intervals as they are used and formed according to the circle of fifths.[35] Perhaps it is also a historical product of the coexistence of rationally and irrationally tuned instruments such as the ch'in.[36]

But the idea of reducing tonal material to the smallest uniform distances rests, as we shall see later, on the purely melodic character of music unacquainted with chordal harmony. The lack of chordal harmony leaves such music without any primary barriers to ascending and descending intervallic measurement. Indeed, wherever music is not rationalized according to chords, the principles of melodic distance and harmonic division are not in conflict. Only fifths and fourths and their difference, the whole tones, are the pure result of the latter. By contrast thirds almost everywhere appear as melodic distance intervals. Testifying to this is the old Arabic tanbur from Khoussan, tuned in the initial tone, second, fourth, fifth, octave. Also, according to tradition, the kithara of the Hellenes was tuned in the initial tone, fourth, fifth, and octave. The designation for the fifth and fourth was simply large and small distance in China. As far as is known, wherever the fifth and fourth appear and where no specific alteration of the tone system occurs, the major second also has been perceived as an important melodic distance. Its universal significance, thus, is based on harmonic provenience, something very different from Helmholtz' tone relationship.[37]

In general the major second has priority over the harmonic third. The ditone, the melodic distance of a third, is by no means an anomaly. Even today there seem to be exceptional cases where in purely melodically conditioned situations the soloist may descend from the harmonic step of a third to the interval of the pythagorean ditone. Despite the harmonically correct measurement of the third by Archytas (in Plato's time) and later by Didymos (who correctly distinguishes between the two whole tones) and still later by Ptolemy, it did not play a revolutionizing role harmonically as in the musical development of the Occident.

Somewhat analogous to the discovery of the geocentric system or the technical qualities of steam power, the harmonic third remained the property of the theorists. The reason for this lies in the character of ancient music which is oriented toward tonal distances and melodic successions of intervals. In practice this makes the third appear as a ditone.

3. TONALITY AND ITS EQUIVALENTS

IN ANCIENT MELODY

Equalization of Scale Intervals in the Interests of Melodic Transposition

The tendency toward the equalizations of distances has been largely determined by interest in the transposition of melodies. Traces of such equalization are preserved in fragments of Hellenic melody such as the second Apollo hymn from Delphi. Hellenic music, for instance, occasionally repeated a tone phrase in different pitch.[1] To make this possible the whole-tone steps had to be of equal dimensions when dealing with such melodically sensitive hearing as that of the Greek. (Thus it is no accident that the harmonically correct measurement of the third did not initially take place with the diatonic but with the chromatic and enharmonic scales from which the ditone was excluded.) The same need for equalization appeared in the early Middle Ages where it implemented mutations into higher or lower hexachords (do–re–mi–fa–sol–la equals the distance scale c–d–e–f–g–a). When exceeding the hexachord ambitus, the steps do–re, re–mi, fa–sol,

sol–la (c–d, d–e, f–g, g–a) had to be regarded as equal whole-tone distances. Precisely here appears the ancient interpretation of the third as a diatonic distance. This is why the quantity of the equal distances was brought to the optimum within the diatonic tonal succession: six fifths, six (and after the acquisition of the chromatic string, seven) fourths, five whole-tone steps, two diatonic and two one-and-one-half–tone steps. Moreover, certain experiments to be mentioned later, with the Arabic scale which was in bad disorder because of irrational thirds, suggest similar motives.

Helmholtz' Theory of Tonality

It is not easy to say precisely what in modern tonality, a tonal system constructed primarily on melodic or distance principles, gives it a firm foundation. The very ingenious formulations in Helmholtz' fine book no longer exactly conform to the available empirical evidence.[2] Even the panharmonicists' assumption that excepting the primitive, all melodicism is finally based on dissected chords, does not smoothly accord with the facts.[3] Only recently has empirical knowledge available through phonograms of primitive music supplied materials for a more adequate picture of origins. This evidence as to the nature of primitive melodicism hardly accords with the supposition that it rests on a strictly naturalistic scale. In Patagonian phonograms, for example, there are latitudes for intonational deviations from a naturalistic scale of up to a halftone. A range of variations is treated as one and the same tone.[4] Only recently has the analysis of the limitless possibilities of musical expressiveness for pure melodicism been cultivated for purposes of advanced study.

The question, finally, of most interest is how far natural tone relationships purely as such have been important as a dynamic element in musical development. Even today this question should be answered for concrete cases only by experts and then with great caution. As indicated by Helmholtz, it may be questioned whether harmonics played a role in the evolution of ancient music.

Primitive Equivalents of Tonality

The assumption must be abandoned that primitive music is a chaos of arbitrariness. The feeling for something corresponding to our tonality is hardly recent. According to Stumpf, Gilmann, Filmoore, O. Abraham, von Hornbostel, and others it appears in many musical pieces of Oriental music.[5] It is known in Hindu music under a special name, Ansa.[6] However, the meaning and function of such tonality equivalents are essentially different and their range is more limited in melodically structured music than in our own.

Primitive melodicism has certain distinct external characteristics. The musical formations of the Vedda, for instance, one of the few people with no musical instruments, not only display rhythmic structuralization, a kind of primitive periodicity of typical cadential and semicadential tones, but also despite the universally strong inclination of the voice toward diatonization, the tendency toward the conservation of the normal tone steps which are, indeed, harmonically irrational and lie between a tempered three-quarter tone and a whole tone.[7] This is not as obvious as it seems to us today. The stepwise nature of tone motion is explained, on the one hand, by the effects of rhythm on tone formation, granting it a shocklike char-

acter, and, on the other hand, by language which must
have been important for the evolution of melody.[8]

The Effects of Language on Ancient Melody

The role of language in the evolution of melody may be
examined briefly. Sometimes it would seem to have no influence, for there are people who, like the Patagonians, sing
their melodies exclusively in nonsense syllables. However,
it has been proved that this was not originally the case.

Generally, articulated language leads to articulated
tone formation. Under special circumstances language
may have other direct influences on melodic formations.
There are tone languages in which the significance of
syllables changes according to the pitches at which they
are pronounced. Chinese is the classic example. Among
the music of phonographically recorded primitives, that
of the Ewe Negroes supplies an example.[9] The melody of
a song in a tone language had to cling to linguistic sense
in a very specific manner, creating distinctly articulated
intervals. The same holds for languages which, though not
tone languages, have so-called "musical accent" (pitch
accent) in contrast to dynamic accent (expirational stem
accent, i.e., raising the tone of the accented syllable rather
than increasing the volume of the tone). This was the
case with classical Greek and, less certainly, with classical
Latin, though the existence of musical accent in classical
Greek is no longer unconditionally beyond dispute.

Of archeological remains of the music of past societies,
the oldest for which a date can be definitely established
follows linguistic accent. This is not true for the others.
As proved by Crusius,[10] the oldest musical fragment, the
hymn of the first Delphic Apollo, follows linguistic ac-

cent; but the similarly archaic Mesemedes hymn does not. Even the Ewe Negroes, with their tone language, do not consistently achieve idiomatic tone motion by means of the melody.[11]

There are strong forces tending to shatter the one-to-one correspondence of language and melody. Musically there is a tendency to repeat the same motive in different words. From the standpoint of language the strophic structure of a song with a fixed tune has to destroy the unity of language and melos. For the Hellenes such unity as existed originally had to disappear with the development of the language into an exquisite rhetorical tool. This development caused the decay of musical accent. In the case of the Ewe Negroes, despite the curtailment of melodicism, which in the long run is only relative in nature and which also occurs in the tone languages, the link of language and melody might have inclined the musical system toward the development of fixed rational intervals. Indeed the occurrence of rational musical intervals seems to be natural to peoples with a tone langauge.

Magical and Sacred Factors in the Range of Primitive Melody

The ambitus (range) of melody is small in all genuinely primitive systems. In most cases, for example in the music of the North American Indians (for whom scalar tone formation as a whole is rather important), there are numerous "melodies" in which a single tone is repeated rhythmically.[12] There are other melodies on two tones. In the music of the Veddas, who had no instruments, the range comprises three tones somewhat similar to a minor third.[13] In the music of the Patagonians, who at least possess the musical bow, which is widely diffused over the world, the range, according to E. Fischer, is extended on exceptional occasions to a seventh though the fifth is the normal maximum.[14] Even in developed musical systems, all ceremonial, hence stereotyped melodies have less range and smaller tone steps.

In the Gregorian chant 70 per cent of all tone progressions are second steps. Even the neumes of Byzantine music, with the exception of four, do not exclusively mean *pneumata* (skips) but *semata* (diatonic tone steps). Byzantine as well as early Occidental church music, the latter at first without exception, kept within the range of an octave and prohibited progressions exceeding a fifth. Similarly, the very antique chorus singing in the synagogues of the Syrian Jews, of which J. Parisot gave a few specimens, strives to keep the range from a fourth to a sixth. Among the Greeks only the Phrygian mode which inherited the characteristic intervallic distance of a sixth ($e-c$) was famous for its extensive skips. Pindar's first Pythian ode, though the available score is certainly of post-classical origin, is kept within the range of a sixth.[15] Hindustani sacred music avoids tonal skips of more than four tones. Similar practices are widespread.

It is probable that in a great many rationalized music systems the fourth is the normal melodic range. In medieval Byzantine theory, for instance, in Bryennies "emmelian tone series" the fourth, which was thought to sound pleasant, was basic.

The Increased Range of Secular Folk Music

Secular folk music very frequently shows a larger range and greater freedom than sacred or ceremonial mu-

sic. This is strikingly true for the music of the Cossacks,
but it also appears elsewhere. Freedom and increased
range are a symptom of greater youth and less stereotyping than is normal for sacred music. The plasticity of secular music also shows an increasing influence of instruments upon music. Yodeling, for instance, with its large
range and use of falsetto, is a recent product probably
originating under influence of horn instruments, as Ho-
henemser proves for the *Kühreihen* (cow round dance)
which developed around a seventeenth century *Waldhorn*.

The characteristics of genuinely primitive music are
found in relative smallness of melodic range, and, often
correlated therewith, a relative largeness of intervals understood as stepwise in nature (not only seconds, but,
according to von Hornbostel, also thirds, and often, indeed, as a consequence of pentatonicism). On the other
hand, relatively small skips occur together (rarely exceeding the interval of a fifth, except for following melodic sections on the occasion of reiteration of the melodic
line). The extension of range and use of rational intervals
occur together, though certainly not everywhere and
alone. Beside the octave the fifth is also employed by
peoples whose primitive instruments (bows) may scarcely
have contributed anything of importance to rationalization. Rationalization has been partly the effect of instruments and has been fixed or supported in its fixing by
them. Indeed, only with the aid of instrumental illustra-
tion can the idea be maintained that the overwhelming
quantity of intervals is rational. This idea appears in
primitive music systems, even in systems which are not
acquainted with the octave but which have forms of instrumental accompaniment. It appears even in such unorganized musical formations as those of the Patagonians.

By providing the accompaniment to the dance, instruments have affected the melodicism of dance songs in ways often of basic importance in music history. With the help of instrumental crutches, tone formation first dared to undertake large steps, at times so extending its range that its steps could only be vocally accomplished with the help of falsetto (as with the music of the Wanyamwesi).[16] Incidentally, falsetto occasionally develops into the general form of singing. On the other hand, by means of instruments, the musician not only learned how to distinguish the consonances with certainty but to fix them unmistakably and consciously use them as artistic devices.

The harmonically most perfect intervals, the octave, fifth, and fourth were distinguished by the recognizability which made them paramount for the development of a primitive tonality. They are distinguished for the musical memory from tone distances near them by their greater clarity. As it is easier correctly to remember real as contrasted to unreal events and clear as contrasted to confused thoughts, a corresponding condition is present for distinguishing right and wrong rational intervals. The analogy between musically and logically rational relations may be extended at least this far.

The majority of ancient instruments contain the simplest intervals as harmonics or as directly neighboring tones. In instruments with movable tuning only the fifth and fourth could be remembered and used as univocal tuning tones.

The phenomenon of measurability of the perfect intervals, once recognized, has been of extraordinary influence on the imagination as shown by the quantity of number mysticisms connected with it.

The Differentiation of Tone Series from Original Magical Formulae

The theoretic differentiation of certain tone series has often occurred in connection with tone formulae typical of most musical systems at an early developmental stage of culture.

Sociologically primitive music appears to a considerable extent to have been removed at an early evolutionary stage from the sphere of pure aesthetic enjoyment and subjected to practical requirements. It was addressed to magical ends, particularly apotropaic (cult) and exorcistic (medicinal) needs.[17] Therewith it was subjected to the stereotyping to which any magically important action or object is inevitably exposed. This holds for works of fine art, mimes or recitations, instrumental or vocal devices (or, often, all of them together) when used for influencing the gods or demons. Since any deviation from a magical formula once proved to be effective destroys its potency, in fact, since such deviation can attract the wrath of metaphysical powers, the exact memorization of the tone formulae was a vital matter. The wrong rendition of a tone formula was an offense which often could be atoned for only through the instantaneous murder of the offender. Once canonized for any reason, stereotyped tone intervals were of extraordinary influence.

Even the instruments which helped in the fixing of the intervals were often differentiated according to the particular god or demon to whom the magical tone formulae were addressed. The Hellenic aulos was originally the instrument of the mother of the gods, later of Dionysus.[18] The oldest keys of the Greek music system also were typical differentiations of tone formulae used in the service of certain gods or at specific festive occasions. Unfortunately there are almost no reliable traditions of really primitive tone formulae of this kind. Precisely the oldest were the objects of secret art which rapidly fell into decay under the contact and influence of modern culture. The ancient inaccessible tone formulae of the Hindu soma sacrifice, which were still known to Haug, seem to be lost for good with the premature death of this scientist. The soma sacrifice is very expensive and disintegrates for economic reasons.

Tone intervals appearing in such magical formulae had in common only the possession of a melodious character throughout. For example, the fact that an interval is used with the descending melody, as, by the way, is still true for traditional contrapuntalism, does not at all prove that it may be used in a descending fashion. As little does the presence of an interval involve the acceptance of the inversion of the interval. The descending melody was considered normal in Hellenic music and is found in the majority of ancient music systems, supposedly due to physiological causes. Most of the time the scale of intervals is highly incomplete and arbitrary from a harmonic standpoint. The scale of intervals does not correspond to Helmholtz' postulate of derivation from tone relationships mediated by partial tones.

Rationalization and Expression and the Professionalization of Music

Rationalization proper commences with the evolution of music into a professional art, be it of sacerdotal or aoidic nature: that is reaching beyond the limited use of tone formulae for practical purposes, thus awakening purely aesthetic needs.

A phenomenon of primitive music which influenced the development of cultured musical systems is the expressive alteration of intervals and, indeed, in contrast to harmonically conditioned music, even by small irrational distances to such a degree that tones which are very close to one another (particularly different kinds of thirds) appear in the same musical structure. It is a major advance when tones lying close together are excluded from simultaneous use. This occurs in Arabian musical practice and also, according to theory, in Hellenic music. It is brought about through the setting up of typical tone series.

Ordinarily this is not done for tonal reasons but for practical reasons.[19] The tones occurring in certain songs had to be put together in a manner permitting the tuning of instruments. This may now react back upon music-making; the melopole is now taught in such a manner that the melody is accommodated to one of these patterns and thus to the corresponding instrumental tuning. In a melodically oriented music these series of intervals do not have the harmonically determined meaning of our present-day keys.

The different keys of Hellenic art music and analogous formations in Hindu, Persian, Eastern-Asiatic music and, in essentially stronger tonal sense, even the church modes of the Middle Ages are, in Helmholtz' terminology, accidental rather than essential scales like ours.[20] They are not, like ours, bordered on top and bottom by a tonic; nor do they represent an essence of triadic tones. In principle they are patterns built according to distance which contain the range and its corresponding admitted tones. First, they can be negatively distinguished from one another in terms of tones and intervals known but not used by the music. On their instruments, the single aulos and potentially, also, the single kithara, at the end of the classical period the Greeks had the full chromatic scale. On the lute the Arabs had all rational and irrational intervals of their tone system. The common scales represented a selection among these available tones. This selection characterized their structure, determined by the position of the semitone steps within the succession of tones and then through the antagonism of certain intervals to each other. For the Arabs the thirds illustrate this.

A tonic in our sense is unknown, for the succession of intervals is not based on a fundament of triads. It rather contradicts triadic comprehension even where the intervals are located within the diatonic tone series. The really genuine Hellenic key, the Dorian, corresponding to the Phrygian church mode (beginning tone e), strongly resists our modern chordal and harmonic tonality.[21] This is immediately evident as soon as one deals with the lowest tone in terms of our tonic. According to our concepts a typical authentic cadence in the Phrygian church mode is impossible due to the fact that the dominant chord b leads to the fifth f-sharp. Thus it contradicts the basic intervallic structure of the Phrygian scale: its beginning with the semitone step e–f. Moreover, it ought to contain as a third the major seventh d-sharp in its function as a leading tone. Its utilization in the Phrygian mode is impossible because it would place the initial tone e, in contradiction with the basic principles of diatonicism, between two semitone steps which follow directly after each other. The place of the dominant can, thus, be taken here only by the subdominant, quite corresponding to the fundamental position of the fourth in most purely melodic tone systems.

From the standpoint of our harmonic concept of music this example illustrates with sufficient clarity the difference between scales of tonal and of intervallic formation. It is quite impossible to find a place for our major and minor in intervallically rationalized music (especially in the old ante-Glarean church modes). Where the final chord in a church mode (for instance the Dorian, after its recognition, the Aeolian mode) ought to have been a minor chord, one concludes with an empty fifth simply because the minor third was not considered to be of sufficient consonance. Thus the final chords ought always to impress us as major chords. This is one of the reasons for the much talked about "major" character of old church music. In fact old church music stands entirely on the other side of this division. Helmholtz already pointed to the fact that one can still observe in J. S. Bach the aversion to conclusions in the minor key, at least in chorales and other tone formations consisting of self-enclosed units.[22]

Ancient Equivalents of Modern Tonality

In the early stages of melodic rationalization, what formed the importance of the tone series? And what corresponded to our tonality in the musical interpretation of the time?

In the language of the Stumpf school, there was orientation around certain main tones, representing a kind of "melodic center of gravity." This is first manifest in the quantitative frequency of sounds and not necessarily in a characteristic qualitative musical function. In almost all really primitive melodies one or sometimes two tones of this kind can be found. In the old ecclesiastical chant the *petteia* (a technical term in Byzantine and archaic stereotyped Armenian church music) [23] is a remnant of the psalmodic uses as well as the repercussion tone (*tonus currens*) of the church modes (which is named in this manner from times past).[24] But even the *mese* of Hellenic music, to be sure, only fragmentarily in available compositions, originally had similar functions. So, too, did the finale in the plagal church modes. In all older music systems the principal tone usually lies somewhere in the middle of the range of the melody. Where fourths organize the tone material, it usually forms the initial point for ascending and descending calculation. It serves as the initial tone in the tuning of instruments and is unalterable at modulations.

The typical melodic formulae are of far greater importance than this central tone. Certain intervals are characteristic for the corresponding key. This was still the case for the church modes of the Middle Ages. To be sure, at times it is difficult to attribute one melody to one church mode and the harmonic attributions of the single tone are ambiguous. The conception of the authentic church modes as a type of octave characterized by its lowest tone is probably a late product of the theory influenced by Byzantine music. But even the practical music of the later Middle Ages still recognized the modal affinities of a melody which to our sensibilities often appear to be a fluctuating quality. This affinity for a given church mode is manifest in three things: the concluding formula, the so-called repercussion interval, and the tropus.

Viewed historically only the concluding formulae in

church music belong to the very early material developed
before the theoretic fixing of the church modes as octave
species. In the oldest church music, so far as conclusions
can be drawn from Armenian music, the interval of the
minor third, common to a great many music systems,
might have been predominant in its function of a recitative-like final cadence. The typical concluding formulae
of the church modes quite correspond to traditions of
music systems which did not lose their tonal fundament
through the influence of virtuosi. Precisely the most primitive music systems have fixed rules for conclusions. Like
most rules in contrapuntalism, they consist less in positive
directions than in the exclusion of certain liberties.

In Vedda music, in contrast to the melodic motion itself, the conclusion never seems to occur in a descending,
but always in an ascending fashion or on the same pitch.
Particularly prohibited was use at the conclusion of the
semitone step which is located above the two normal
tones of the melody. One may observe in Vedda music
how, beginning with an organized finale, regulation is
extended backward. The final cadence comes to be anticipated by a rather extensive typical penultimate cadence observing similarly fixed rules.

The development for an original melodicism starting
from the coda is also probable in the synagogue chant as
well as in church music.[25] The final tone is often regulated
in music systems which are still quite irrational. As many
contemporary phonograms show, the final and half cadence on the melodic principal tone are frequently the
rule. Where there is a different interval, fourths and fifths
relations stand out distinctly. Von Hornbostel beautifully
illustrated this with Wanyamwesi songs where the principal tone often has an uptone or several of this kind, the

latter of which are felt as leading toward it.[26] In music systems with predominantly descending melodies it is located underneath the principal tone. According to von Hornbostel it can form various regular intervals up to a major third. As compared with the harmonic leading tone which is always located on the semitone step underneath the tonic, the position of this uptone in purely melodic music systems offers a colorful picture. Alongside the tendency of the melody to descend is the fact that tuning is also easier moving down from above.

The rationalized scales of stringed instruments have small tone steps, like the Dorian fourth of the Greeks, sometimes in the neighborhood of the lower frame tone of its tonic, which is characterized by pseudo-Aristotle [27] as leading distinctly to the hypate. It is therefore very hard to sustain as an independent tone in singing. The Arabic conjunct scale of fifths experimented later with three different kinds of neighboring tones underneath g and c', thus with upper uptones. In the Chinese scale the degradation of the semitone to an unsatisfactory tone step is also evident. This is perhaps the case in other pentatonic scales as a product of the sense of "lack of independence" caused by its melodically leading position.

When musical development attributes the role of a melodic uptone to the semitone stem, neither this nor the development toward a leading tone is of an entirely general nature. The occurrence of the uptone despite the general avoidance belongs here. Sometimes purely melodic music tends toward an uptone. The existence of typical uptone intervals as certainly as the development of final cadences is being brought into a tonal organization of tone intervals in relation to the principal tone in its function as a tonic. An example is provided by the church modes.

Purely melodic music systems in the course of the development into a virtuoso art are led in precisely the opposite direction, abolishing predispositions for fixed final cases. If von Hornbostel is right, such are already found in Wanyamwesi music. Virtuoso development also threatens the role of the principal tone. Hellenic music during its early history had something corresponding to the best of our final cadences (a second, but most of the time a major lower second and minor upper second before the final note). A typical cadential tone, even if not especially employed throughout, is to be observed for subdivisions (verse endings) too. The final tone then joins the frame tones of fourths forming the basis of the scale.

However many other music systems such as the Eastern-Asiatic art music systems hardly know of such a thing. They terminate quite negligently not only with the second of the initial tone, which frequently plays a kind of harmonic role in its function as a principal melodic interval constituted through fourth and fifth, but with any other interval. In Hellenic music the tonal type is less clear the more melodically refined the musical structure. One can observe in Hellenic and in primitive as well as art music systems that with peculiar frequency half cadences are a rather rhythmic phenomenon. There frequently appear extensions of tonal time values as found in most primitive music systems. Such formations played an important role in Occidental musical development both in the synagogues and in the churches.

Less consistently was the principle realized only temporarily and soon modified in the old church modes that the composition had to begin with the final note (accord-

ing to Wilhelm von Hirsau) or with an interval harmonically related to it (in the eleventh century: the fifth,
fourth, and later the third or second, but, in any case no
more distant tone from the final one than the fifth).

So far as may be determined by the archeological
remains, Hellenic music shows nothing of the sort. Other
music systems show most varied traditions. Beginnings
with a minor second of the final tone are found (in Arabic
and some Asiatic systems). Some primitive systems begin
their melodies in the octave (as in that of the Ewe Negroes) or one of the dominants. In church composition
musical seconds form the principal seat of the tropes.
The latter were originally melodic formulae memorized
according to syllables which characteristically contained
the repercussion intervals of the key. In this case they are
not primitive. Moreover, like all the musical systems of
Christendom, they never had magical significance.

Finally, the repercussion interval itself was very frequent in the corresponding melodies. It was proper to
any church mode and resulted from the range and structure provided by the position of the semitone steps. It was
frequent at a time when the church modes were already
rationalized on Byzantine models into four authentic keys
which ascended from d, e, f, and g as final tones of the
octave and into four plagal keys which started with the
same final tones but which were placed between the lower
fourth and upper fifth.

In the authentic modes the repercussion tone was at
the fifth with the exception of the Lydian which started
with f. In the Lydian mode it was the sixth. In the plagal
modes it was twice the fourth, one the major and one the
minor third, always counting from the final tone. The intervals seem to have been determined by the fact that the

lower of both tones of the halftone interval of the key
was avoided as an upper tone of the repercussion interval.
This is to be considered less a fragment from pentatonicism than a symptom of the role of the lower semitone
which was felt as leading.

Even the tropes which were accepted by the church be-
latedly and with hesitation are analogous to the schemata
by Byzantine music, perhaps borrowed from it, the theory
of which, indeed distinguished a whole series of melodic
formulae. A diffusion of the old Hellenic music system
was occurring. This was perhaps due to Oriental (Hebrew)
influence the direction of which, unfortunately, cannot be
established. But development hardly reverted to the formulae of Hellenic musical practice. In olden times the
latter might have worked with fixed melodic formulae.
This is doubtful, probable though it may seem. In any
case nothing can any longer be proved. Reliance on
sacred tone formulae of a pagan cult in ecclesiastical
music was in principle excluded.

The parallel influences upon synagogue music cannot
be certainly determined. Synagogue music also developed
tropes, and it agrees in a number of melodic clausulae with
parts of the Gregorian chant. However, at least in its new
creations it relied to the highest degree upon traditional musical practices of the milieu. From the eighth to
the thirteenth century in the Occident it was predominantly influenced by the Gregorian chant and by folk
melodicism. In the Orient in contrast to the Hellenic area
it was influenced in a limited manner by Persian-Arabic
music. As mentioned earlier, its scales correspond essentially to the church modes of the Middle Ages.

4. SCALE RATIONALIZATION IN TERMS

OF FIFTHS AND FOURTHS: FOUN-

DATIONS OF MODERN TONALITY

Role of Fourths and Fifths in Melodic Transposition

THOSE intervals appearing in music systems which
have been rationalized and are regularly found in temperament are the fifths and fourths. In Japanese and other
art music systems and already in Negro music, modulations or transpositions of the center of gravity preferably
occur in the position of the fifth or fourth. The songs of
the Ewe Negroes show distinctive thematic organization
rather than variation of the same motive which usually
predominates.[1] Rather unorganized repetition of the same
motive in the fourth appears to be characteristic of the
original transposition problem which is of such importance
from a developmental and a historical standpoint.

However, the existence of a melodic tonality of fourths
and fifths and even an elaboration of triads does not prevent the appearance of irrational chromatic single tones
(as for the Ewe Negroes) besides those modulations

which are normal to our sensibilities. Its appearance in a
music system even where it has harmonic character and
where fifth and fourth are the accompanying intervals in
the many-voiced singing does not necessarily imply its
universal rationalization. Quite the contrary. There are
circumstances where the most irrational intervals are to
be found beside them as bearers of harmony, as we shall
see later.

The intervals of the fifth and fourth belong together.
They are inversions of one another, appearing partly in co-
operation, dividing their work between them, partly in
competition. Generally the fourth is the fundamental
melodious interval while the fifth is often the basis of instrumental tuning. However, next to the tetrachord the
pentachord is found. Though occasionally, as in Arabia,
the consonant quality of the fifth has been doubted under
influence of the tonality of the fourth.

The competition between the intervals also appears in
the development of European music, being terminated
only when the fifth found re-enforcement through the
third. In the theory of many-voiced music of the Middle
Ages this ended with the degrading of the fourth to a
dissonance. As a main interval, the fourth was more important in Byzantine and old Hellenic music than in the
church modes with their strong orientation toward the
fifth. In the church modes the plagal secondary keys
from the dominant (lower fourth equals fifth) of the principal key and at least three of the authentic keys have
fifths as main intervals while, by contrast the plagal keys
which were probably imported from the Orient and in
which the fourth is located below, avoid skips of a fifth.

Old Hellenic theory formed the series of secondary keys
(the "hypo" keys) from the subdominant (lower fourth

equals fifth). If the phonographic reproductions of many primitive tones are correct (the tendency of the voice to distone, which was mentioned, is the only reason to doubt it) the diatonic intervals, especially the fourth, fifth, and whole tone, would appear in correct size in music systems with less than an octave range. (This seems to be the case for the Patagonians who, according to travelers' reports, have a phenomenal ability for instantaneous imitation of European melodies.)

Such facts would seem to suggest that the fourth is historically the first, the octave the last of the three main consonances to be discovered. However, this is not established for certain. Attempts to explain the development of the Hellenic music system in this manner are premature. Indeed, the interpretation of the Hellenic music system must include not only, as in other purely melodic systems, the arithmetic division of the octave by the fourth as the proper equal division (according to pseudo-Aristotle [2]) but the elevation of the fifth to the significance of a fundamental interval (occasionally ascribed to Pythagoras [3]). This may have led to the rationalization of the octave which is dissected into two diazeutic fourths [4] separated by the tonus from which any one tone of the fourth (for instance, e – a) is kept in the distance of a fifth for the corresponding tone of the other (b–e), thus the fixing of instrumental tuning by means of the circle of fifths.

Origin of the Keys in Rationalization of Melodic Formulae

The manner in which the three-stringed kithara was originally tuned remains uncertain.[5] More important, as in Hellas, is the origin of the various keys through rationalization of typical melodic formulae. This is hardly questionable even though nothing other than the pattern of names (Dorian, Phrygian, etc.) remains from their history. These typical melodic formulae were employed in the religious service of various deities. They were specific church tones, finding their school-like development in nonreligious lyrical and elegiac writing (singing accompanied by lyre and flutes).

Hypotheses will be advanced later as to the probable role of instruments on such occasions. It is difficult to determine the status of the generally accepted tone successions preserved in complicated Hellenic scale doctrine. Either these consisted of tone successions of intervals within octave range, the series being determined by the position of the semitones starting from any of the seven tones of a diatonic octave (by range extension over the octave to two octaves) or the tone succession consisted of a regrouping of the intervals within the same octave by means of a different tuning of the instruments.

Though the details are of no concern we are interested in the inner tensions of this tone system. Once the octave had been made the basis of the tonal system, the circle of fifths as the theoretic basis of tuning, on the one hand, and the fourth as a melodic fundamental interval, on the other, had to come into tension. Thereafter the continuous growth of the melodic range inevitably led to a dynamic interplay precisely at the place where it also appears for modern harmony: at the unsymmetrical construction of the octave.

The Dorian mode, which descended from the middle tone (*mese*) a, and ascended from the secondary middle tone (*paramese*) b to A or a' respectively, thus contained, according to Aristotle, the normal range of the human voice, a tone series of two octaves and proceeding in a diatonic fashion.[6] In post-classical times this Dorian tone series was considered to be the fundamental scale of tones. It probably also has been the fundamental scale historically. Descending from e to B and ascending from e′ to a′ it contained symmetric fourths consisting of the middle fourth e–a and of the diazeutic fourth b–e′. Each fourth had the initial tone in common with the preceding tone. It stood in the relationship of synaphe or fourth relationship of the parallel tones. In response to the unsymmetrical construction of the octave the middle fourth e–a was in diazeutic relation or fifths of the parallel tones with respect to the diazeutic fourth b–e′. The frame tones of the fourth, thus, B, e, a, b, e′, a′ and the lower additional tone (proslambanomenos) A, were considered to be fixed. They were tones which could not be tuned to a different key or tone gender.

In other music systems, too, the frame tones of the fourths were treated as immovable, the other tones as movable melodic elements. Properly speaking, regular modulation (metabole) into different tone genders or into different keys (fourth relationship) ought only to have occurred by crossing these fixed tones. The lack of symmetry of the division was evident. A tone series standing in synaphe (fourth relationship) and in symmetric relationship with the middle fourth, could only be obtained in an ascending fashion through the introduction of the tone b-flat next to b. This led to the addition of the chromatic b-flat string on the kithara.

The term chromatic had essential significance in this case as in harmonic music, for it expressed a tonal condition, not merely a relation of tone distance. The use of the b-flat string was interpreted as a modulation (in Hel-

lenic terminology the *agoge peripheres*) into another
tetrachord a, b-flat, c', d' conjoined (synemmenon)
through the *mese* (a) with the middle fourth (e – a) and
in symmetric relation with the diazeutic fourth b, c, d, d'.
Thus, tonally speaking, the modulation was interpreted
as going from the fifth to the fourth relation.

The series of conjunct fourths reaches its end at d'. The
step b-flat–b could obviously not be an admitted tonal
step, but in order to use the b-flat string, one had to
ascend from the *mese* a, which realized the modulation
into one of the two fourths (a, b-flat, c', d', or b, c', d',
e'). Then one had to descend in the other fourth back to
the *mese*. At least this was the case in strict theory.

Obviously the true motive for the construction of the
synemmenon is simply given by the fact that in the diatonic scale, which the Hellenes also accepted as normal,
F is the only tone which, due to asymmetry of the division
of the octave, has no fourth above it, the fourth being the
basic interval of the melodicism of nearly all ancient
music.

Parallel Developments in Other Music Systems

The correlation of the fourths and fifths, expressed in
the combination of diazeutic and conjunct tetrachords, is
found not only in Hellenic music but in Javanese and in
somewhat changed form in Arabian music.

The theory of the Arabic scales of the Middle Ages,
which due to errors of Villoteau and Kiesewetter,[7] seem
to be extremely confused, have been put upon a more
plausible, though perhaps not more secure, basis by Collangettes.[8] Under Hellenic influence before the tenth century the fourths were divided downward and upward in

pythagorean fashion, thus containing five tones each: c, d, e-flat, e, f; f, g, a-flat, a, b (d, e, a from below, e-flat and a-flat assessed from above).[9] In the tenth century the fourths had absorbed two different species of neutral thirds, which resulted in seventeen, in part completely irrational, intervals of the octave. This will be discussed later.

If Collangettes is right, in the thirteenth century both fourths were rationalized by the theory in such way that one, also to be discussed more completely later, retained the third contained next to it. In each fourth was contained, likewise, one irrational second, which was separated from it by a pythagorean tone step. Moreover, the intervals between these neutral and pythagorean relations were reduced to the range of residual pythagorean intervals. Thus they were included in the scheme of tonal formation by the numbers 2 and 3. The lower of both fourths now contained the following tones (reduced to c): pythagorean d-flat, irrational d, pythagorean e-flat, irrational e, pythagorean e, f, with six distances of: limma, limma, apotome, limma, apotome minus the limma, limma. The rational d was canceled. One did not yet dare to exclude the harmonic fifth g. The upper fourth, on the contrary, contained the following tones: f, pythagorean g-flat, irrational g, harmonic g, pythagorean a-flat, irrational a, pythagorean a, harmonic b and harmonic g, pythagorean a-flat, irrational a, pythagorean a, harmonic b and the seven distances of limma, limma, apotome minus limma, limma, limma, apotome minus limma, limma. Ascending, standing next to the conjunct fourth within the octave the whole tone step remained with which a new conjunct system of fourths started. The lower fourth con-

tained three, the upper fourth four overlapping whole-
tone steps.

The question which of the two fourth positions, the
fourth or fifth tonality, is the older, cannot be answered
with certainty. It can only be answered probably in favor
of the fifth, thus of the diazeutic fourth. This applies at
least to music based on and starting from the octave. In
primitive music the fourth could have obtained its importance merely through melodic procedures. The Javanese system of conjunct fourths (if the pelog system can
be interpreted in such a way) was probably imported
from Arabia. It can no longer be ascertained whether
tetrachords ever played a role in structuring the octave
in Chinese music. However, in Hellas the chromatic string,
thus the conjunct fourth, was added later according to
tradition and notation. This may have been the case wherever the conjunct pattern of fourths appeared alongside
the disjunct one. It appeared here for the first time when,
under the influence of instruments, the ambitus of tones
utilized was extended beyond the octave and at the same
time descending and ascending conjunct fourths emerged
unsymmetrically next to two disjunct fourths of the starting octave. In reaction, the sense for symmetry led to
striving for the transposability of melodies into other
pitch levels. This was of great importance in music history.
Precisely the same procedure, the insertion of a single
chromatic tone, took place in Hellas as well as in medieval
Europe under the same inclinations and on the same type
of material. In Byzantine music, in order to transpose
melodies into the fifth in the third ἦχος (Phrygian), one
had to lower b to b-flat. Thus our b corresponded to the
so-called ἦχος βαρύς. The same procedure was to be found
in the Occident. But the manner and direction in which

the urge for symmetry became practically effective deviated from those of antiquity. The special vehicle of this was the solmisation scale.

Role of Solmisation in Occidental Musical Development

Solmisation is a tonal alphabet characterized not by an order of tones *per se,* but by the relative position of tone steps, especially of semitone steps in the scale pattern. At all times, including the present, this pattern in the Occident served the purpose of vocal practice in scale instruction. Something corresponding to their tetrachord genders was known to the Hellenes. There were also parallels in India.

In the schola of Guido d'Arezzo ecclesiastical singing practice of the Middle Ages used, basically, a diatonic and hexatonic scale.[10] Only since the seventeenth century was the heptachord gradually transformed into a heptatonic scale by adding the seventh syllable (si) after it had performed the essential part of its role and was about to become a simple abstract tone designation with the Romans (Italians) and English. This could only have occurred within a single diatonic scale which could not be transposed, divided unsymmetrically by the semitone step. It could not be a quarter-tone scale as in antiquity, for though the position of the fourths remained important, especially in theory, it declined more than in antiquity through the reduction in importance of the antique kithara which had been the historical vehicle of the tetrachord in musical practice and education. The monochord was substituted for the kithara as a school instrument. Moreover, musical education at first concentrated entirely

on singing. It is convincingly argued by H. Riemann that
the attempt was made to find the largest series of tones
which appeared more than once within the diatonic scale.
A homogeneous, symmetrical divisibility was achieved by
means of the semitone step. But this is a hexatonic scale
starting from C or G. In either case it is exactly divisible
in the center through the semitone step. As is known, the
syllables do, re, mi, sol, la—wherein mi–fa always marks
the semitone step—were taken out of the hemistichs of a
St. John's hymn [11] which were ascending diatonic steps.
However the symmetrical hexatonic scales, starting from
C and G respectively, were jointed by the third hexachord
starting from F. Even Guido d'Arezzo, who as strict ad-
herent of diatonicism refused all chromaticism in musical
practice, in order to build a fourth from F, took over the
tone b-flat, "the b-moll," in contrast to and beside the
b-quadratum (b). Though perhaps unintentionally in
practice this very tetrachord symmetry was not confronted
and displaced by the hexachord symmetry precisely because it accepted the chromatic tone.

Emergence of the Tonic, Dominant, and Subdominant of the C-major Scale

Arising out of melodic interests and certainly without
conscious intention, tonic, dominant, and subdominant of
our C-major scale became the starting points of the three
hexachords. This, of course, was not without consequences
for the evolution of modern tonality. It was, indeed, not
the decisive fact, for the b-moll (b-flat) itself arose as a
concession to the old supremacy of the fourth, to which
the small seventh refers back as much as the big seventh
leads on to the octave. The b-flat in itself could have

operated in favor of the fourth's tonality and the "middle-tone system." [12]

That this did not occur was due to decisive peculiarities of musical development in Western civilization, for which the selection of a hexachord pattern was certainly more a symptom than an operating cause. As one factor (beside many others), it was subject to the inner logic of tone relations which immediately pushed on toward the formation of the modern scales the moment the old tetrachord division, resting on the principle of distance, was abandoned at any point.

The superior role of the fourths and fifths in ancient music, discernible everywhere, certainly rests on the role played by the single meaning of their consonance in the tuning of instruments with movable tones. The third could not have performed this role since the older instruments with fixed tones either had none or had only neutral thirds. This is the case for most horns, the flutes, and the bagpipe, with one important exception to be mentioned later (indeed, one of the oldest instruments known in northern Europe).

Generally the reason why of the two intervals the fourth gained ascendancy over the fifth is that it represented the smaller of the intervals. Of course, different explanations were sought for its original predominance and later recession before the fifth. [13] It has been said to occur physically by the mere vocal character of the older polyphonic music. It was maintained that in singing the higher of the two voices tends to monopolize the melody, forcing the lower to adjust itself melodically to it, on the fourth. Thus the fourth harmonic tone of the lower voice coincided with the third tone of the higher. This is said

to be the closest relationship of tones situated in such a
way within the octave (tetrachord tonality).

In contrast, for instrumental two-part writing, the lower
voice is said to have stronger resonance and the upper
tone is said to adjust itself harmonically in the fifth, at
which the third harmonic tone of the lower voice coincides with the second tone of the upper voice (scale
tonality). This explanation, the value of which only experts are entitled to judge, seems historically problematic
since it presupposes polyphony. On the other hand, in
unaccompanied two-part singing of persons completely
devoid of musical training, fifths appear habitually and
easily. Moreover, the Arabic music system does not favor
this position, for though especially rich in instruments,
within it development of the fourth progresses always
toward division in a descending fashion at the expense of
the fifth. Hindustan development would rather support
it. Yet, again, the ascendency of the fourth in the church
modes, in contrast to Hellenic music, occurred despite
the far-reaching repression of instruments.

Apparently the nature of the instruments may have
been an element. On the other hand, the explanation is
certainly tenable for the importance of the instrumental
bass and descending structuration of harmony promoted
by it. At the same time, the position of the fourth in
ancient music can be explained in this manner only with
respect to the peculiar structure of ancient melodies.
These achieve a descending melody and incline toward
the use of the fourth as finale of a melodic phrase. Of
course, this has nothing to do with a stronger resonance
of a higher voice. Even from a purely melodic point of
view, a phrase descending in one stretch down the scale
of passing tones to the fifth (namely C–F), involves a

very long and melodically difficult tritone dissonance if the semitone stands near the end or beginning. Thus, the insertion of a semitone in its center had a significant effect only when the third was already understood harmonically, as today in our tonal organization perhaps the phrase G to C.

As long as the third, in intervallic terms, was felt as a ditone, the fourth was the first clear consonance reached through melodic motion. When the octave was known, it always appeared together with the fifth. For nearly all people, at least those who did not know the third, it was perceived among the intervals as a melodic skip which was especially easy to intone. Moreover, the fact that it was also the smallest unambiguously consonance-making interval in contrast to the ambiguity of the third, finally decided in its favor. Thus it was taken as a starting point for rational intervallic division in musical systems which obtained tone material in accordance with the intervallic principle.

As soon as the ancient types of tone formulae of sacred and medicinal character, which had served as strong tonal supports, are stripped away, the once firmly rooted tonal anchorage comes into continuous fluctuation in a purely melodically developed music. Under the growing need for expressiveness the destruction of all tonal barriers is more complete the more the ear is developed to melodic refinements. Such is the case in Hellenic music. We observe how the chromatic string, as part of a specially conjunct tetrachord, and the fixing of the frame tones of the tetrachords limited, in a theoretically strict manner, the means of modulation. Something corresponding to the musical practice involving instruments, though not strictly proved, can be found insinuated here and there. Many of the observations of writers on music and, even more, archeological remains, especially the first Delphic Apollo hymn indicate that musical practice had little correspondence to theory.[14] Although they should in principle have been rejected, as Gevaert's untiring efforts show, chorus songs were preserved with partly genuinely ancient, partly intentional archaism of simple melodicism.[15] In theory these are at best, capable of rationalization. They hardly correspond to our comprehension of harmony. The first Pythian ode of Pindar (the composition of which cannot be placed in time), the hymns of Mesomedes and, moreover, the little funeral song to Seikolos, presumably imitating popular tunes, can be fitted into the theory fairly well. By contrast, the second great Apollo hymn, belonging to the second century B.C. (even if Riemann's hypothesis of the mutilation of one note symbol be accepted) defies rationalization.[16] The tetrachord theory of the Hellenes limited melodic chromaticism so narrowly that two intervals of main tones could not appear in immediate succession to each other. According to Aristoxenus this was due to the fact that otherwise proportions of the consonances within the fourth patterns would be lost.[17] However, the Apollo hymn contains three successive chromatic intervals and only by assuming extremely free modulations could it be theoretically interpreted with the assistance of Gevaert's explanation that tetrachords of intervally different structure (and of entirely different genders) are here combined with each other.[18] Without doubt an ancient theorist would have construed the circumstances in the same way. The theory of Arabic music approves of similar things, combining differently structured tetrachords and pentachords. Then, according to the circumstances every tonal fourth and fifth relationship in the Hellenic sense, with the exception of the frame tones of the tetrachords, had to be abandoned and a melodicism developed which, despite its lawfulness, was to a large extent detached. Its relation to its musical foundation was as theoretically loose as that of modern music to strict chordal harmonic theory discussed at the beginning of this study.

Precisely official Athenian music (a song of praise to God after the defense against an attack launched by the Celts) is here brought into question. It appears that in Hellenic art music during the period of its greatest creativity the very striving for expressiveness led to an extremely melodic development which shattered the harmonic elements of the system. Since the end of the Middle Ages in the Occident, the same striving led to an entirely different result, the development of chordal harmony. This is to be ascribed, in the first instance, to the fact that at the time the increased demand for expressiveness was felt, the Occident, in contrast to antiquity, was already in possession of polyvoiced music. Expressiveness could then follow the path of polyvoiced music. However, though this is true without any doubt, polyvocality was by no means found only in Occidental music. Thus, its evolutionary conditions must be examined.

5. THE EVOLUTION OF OCCIDENTAL

POLYVOCALITY

Meaning and Forms of Polyvocality

Here in its broadest sense music will be called poly-voiced only when the several voices do not go together exclusively in unison or in the octave. Unison of instruments and voices was known to nearly all musical systems. It was familiar in antiquity. Similarly the accompaniment of voices in octaves (the voices of men, boys, and women) is naturally a very general phenomenon, also familiar to antiquity. Wherever it appeared the octave was perceived as tone identity on another step. Only in its extreme form does polyvoiced music take on typically different character. Of course all kinds of transitional conditions are possible. Their pure types are sharply differentiated from each other. Moreover, historically they have quite different roots even in very primitive musical systems.

Polysonority

One may distinguish, first, modern chordal harmonic polysonority, or, perhaps more strictly, polyvoicedness.

Chord progressions should not necessarily be understood as a quantity of voices, one to be distinguished from the other, and as voices which progress together. On the contrary, the chord progressions do not necessarily even contain in themselves the melodic progressions of a single voice.

The absence of all and any melodicism in the usual sense is, of course, a pure type. This pure type and what musically approximates it has no analogies whatsoever in the music of non-Occidental peoples in the past before the eighteenth century. The Oriental nations, especially those with developed art music, are acquainted with the simultaneous sounding of several tones. Moreover, as mentioned earlier, it appears that at least the major third has been accepted as beautiful by most people whose music lacks tonality in our sense, or, as in the case of the Siamese, whose music rests on a completely different base.[1] Yet such people do not interpret the chord harmonically nor enjoy it as a chord in our way, but as a combination of intervals which they want to hear separately. Thus, they prefer to play them in the form of arpeggios in the same manner as they originated on the harp (*arpa*) and other ancient strummed string instruments. In this form the chord is very anciently known to all peoples possessing instruments with several strings.

Even when the piano was improved in the eighteenth century, the beauty of the sound of arpeggio chords customary from lute performance was one of the effects sought and appreciated. Series of bismorous formations and triads on the harp between the alternating solo and choral parts are to be found in the very fascinating semi-dramatic recitations of legends of the Bantu Negroes recorded by P. H. Trilles.[2] Of course these (very simple)

chord sequences bear no relation to our harmonic progressions. In most cases they came together in unison or,
if not, they conclude under certain circumstances in strong
dissonances (for example the tritone when the reproduction is exact). Fullness of sound seems to have been the
essential goal.

Contrapuntal Polyphony

Another pure type is represented by the form of polyvocality called polyphony which found its consistent type
in contrapuntal writing. Several voices of equal standing
run side by side, harmonically linked in such a way that
the progression of each voice is accommodated to the progression of the other and is, thus, subject to certain rules.

In modern polyphony these rules are partly those of
chordal harmony, partly they have the artistic purpose of
bringing about such a progression of voices that each single one can independently come to its melodic right. Still,
and possibly because of it, the ensemble as such preserves
a strict musical (tonal) uniformity.

Thus, pure chordal harmony thinks musically in two-
dimensional terms: vertically across the staff lines and at
the same time horizontally alongside these lines. Contrapuntalism first operates monodimensionally in horizontal
direction and only then vertically, for the chords were not
born out of configurations constructed uniformly and
from chordal harmonies, but arose, so to speak, by chance
out of the progressions of several independent voices, re-
quiring harmonic regulation. The contrast appears to be
and is largely relative.

How clearly this can be perceived can be demonstrated
not so much by the angry reactions of Italian musical per-

ception of the late Renaissance against the barbarousness
of counterpoint in contrast to harmonic homophonic music, as by the position which was still taken by contrapun-
talists like Grell (manager of the *Singakademie* of Berlin) who in the last third of the nineteenth century flung
his condemnation posthumously against all musical innovations since J. S. Bach.[3] Occasionally his pupil Bellerman
also takes the same position.[4]

However, modern creative artists, oriented to chords,
experience a notable difficulty in the interpretation of
Palestrina and Bach in the same musical sense as their
contemporaries. In spite of all the preparatory stages,
polyphony in this sense, especially contrapuntalism, has
been known in the West in highly developed conscious
form only since the fifteenth century. It attained its highest perfection in the work of Bach.

No other epoch and culture was familiar with it, not
even, as Westphal believed because of wrongly interpreted sources, the Hellenes.[5] So far as is known the Hellenes even completely lacked initial stages similar to those
of the Western world which can be found with most different peoples of the earth.[6] For the Hellenes the words
for the chord as well as for any simultaneous use of the
consonance in music was ἡ συμφωνία οὐκ ἔχει ἦθος that is to
say, having the same meaning. This can be seen, to, in a
passage of pseudo-Aristotle, indicating that consonance
chords were known through the tuning of instruments.[7]
To the Greeks they were pleasant to the ear but had no
musical significance.

This was intended for art music. Naturally it does not
prove that the chord was unknown to the Hellenes. The
contrary can be observed in the remarks of the theorists
about the κρᾶσις of tones with consonances in contrast to

dissonances. Though the assumption is frequently made that in Hellas many-voiced singing occurred in the primitive form of consonance parallels, this can neither be proved nor disproved with certainty. If it occurred the music and chord use must have been folk music (which we naturally cannot trace) and would have belonged to the kind of country fair entertainment of the *crapule*, the musical needs of whom were haughtily dismissed by Aristotle.

Briefly, the artistic means of a specific polyphonic many-voicedness must be recalled. The uniformity of a melodious configuration, polyphonic in a technical sense, has been preserved in its simplest form in the canon: the simple coexistence of the same motive on different steps, having been successively taken over by new voices before expiring in one voice. This singing practice is found in simple folk music as well as in art music. The first preserved example, of course far from the oldest in the Western world, to be dated with certainty in terms of its notation is the famous summer canon of the Monk of Reading (manuscript from the middle of the thirteenth century).[8] By contrast one of the most sublimated art forms of contrapuntalism, the fugue, belongs exclusively to art music. In its simplest form a given theme is imitated by a *comes* (companion) on another pitch (normally fifth). The *comes* in turn is confronted on the initial steps with a counter subject. By means of episodes this game of conflicting forces is interrupted and varied by changes in tempi and (normally, key-related) modulations. By the *stretta* (canon-like entrance of the *comes* next to the theme itself) and also, especially preferably, close to the conclusion of leading the voices over a sustained tone (organ point), the musical meaning of the configuration is concentrated and emphasized. The beginnings of the fugue are ancient. It reached its fullest development only in the seventeenth and eighteenth centuries. Also, outside both these marginal forms, which in a certain sense, are highly characteristic, the either stricter or freer imitation of a given motive on other pitch levels is the vital element of polyphony as art music. This melodious motive is continuously augmented and interpreted ever more intensively from all sides.

Although it has essential beginnings, the evolution of "imitation" to this predominant position is an artistic device belonging only to the fifteenth century. As a second *ars nova* it displaces the coloristic style of the fourteenth century which was an older, more mechanical mode of voice leading. Only since the re-establishment of the papal chapel in the fifteenth century after termination of the schism has contrapuntalism dominated all many-voiced forms of ecclesiastical vocal art. To a considerable extent it has also dominated artistic composition of folk songs since the sixteenth century.[9]

Starting with a simple two-part setting written in *punctus contra punctum* musical development led to compositions of several dozens of voices with two, three, and four notes of one voice against one of the others. It progressed from simple to multiple counterpoint (to a counterpoint formed through reversible voices, one against others). Many-voiced composition had to be woven into an increasingly sublimated and complicated structure in terms of increasingly complex artistic rules.

Even before the appearance of these complicated tasks, the simple problems of parallel motion, lateral motion, counter motion of voices with their rules and prohibitions formed the specific object of a theory of polyvocality

which was gradually developed since the twelfth century.[10] Two prohibitions were of paramount interest, the
one dating at least since the twelfth century (but probably earlier) the other since the fourteenth century. These
were the avoidance of the tritone (the augmented fourth,
if measured in pythagorean terms, e.g., f–b) which since
the Middle Ages was regarded as the sum total of all evil
and ugliness and the prohibition of parallel motions on
perfect consonances, especially of octaves and fifths.

The rigorous prohibition of what is certainly the acute
dissonance of the tritone (which according to Helmholtz'
theory belongs to intervals disturbed by especially close
overtones) which belongs as a specific interval to the
Lydian mode (starting from F) was still unknown to the
genuine Gregorian chorale. Moreover, it did not penetrate
to places where the authority of the church remained relatively weak (as in Iceland).[11] The use of the Lydian
mode was quite familiar to older church music. Later it
was prohibited, at least in its pure form. No church
chorale uses it. One could be tempted to attribute the
origin of this prohibition to the invasion of the Hellenic
tetrachord system into Western music theory since Carolingian times, though of course not in the form of genuine
Hellenic art practice of classical and post-classical times
which did not by any means, as proved by archaeological
remains, avoid the tritone even as a direct skip.[12]

Perhaps the interpretations of tonality in the latest period were influenced by Christians and therefore indirectly by the Orient. Moreover, outside our harmonic
world, which has become accustomed to the tritone step,
it does not seem to be easily intonable. A series of three
whole-tone steps is also avoided as a melodic harshness
by otherwise entirely different musical systems, without

this determining the role played by tonal perceptions and the effect of acquaintance with the fourth.

Once the differentiation between whole tones and semi-tones is clearly learned, it is understandable that a systematic change should occur in both. The whole tone and the semitone or two whole tones and one semitone are now perceived as more pleasant and normal melodically. Considered rationally it was obvious to regard the tritone (and its inversion, the diminished fourth) as an interval cutting the relationship of the fourth and fifth. It destroyed tonality in the meaning this had at the time, namely, the division of the octave into fourths and fifths. For the same reason, Byzantine music did not consider the infraction of the mete (highest note) of the scale by the semitone step as a modulation, like other infractions of the ambitus, but as a destruction of tonality itself.

However, it is possible that the change of the tritone occurred not only later, but parallel with the appearance of polyvocality. Yet, reliable knowledge as to the stages in the historical prohibition has not been obtained. Since the tritone was not allowed to appear simultaneously or successively, neither indirectly nor as a tone series within the ensemble of voices, its prohibition (in medieval language the rule that *mi contra fa* is not permissible) was indeed a very perceptible barrier. A rational explanation was not sought for the fact that although the large intervals, the minor sixth (the main interval of the Phrygian mode) and the octave, even if only as an ascending interval, were allowed, at least by later music theory, yet the major sixth, in contrast to the seventh which always remained forbidden, has never been admitted as a melodic tone step in spite of its good intonation.

We are inclined to account for the often cited prohibi-

tion of fifth and fourth parallels under the dominance of
choral and harmonic music in tonal terms by the fact that
empty fifths and octaves are interpreted by our ear as
fragments of triads. Thus their use is understood as an
uninterrupted change of keys. Polyphony understood in
purely melodic terms would reject this usage for a different reason, as a threat to the musical independence of the
single voices with respect to each other. As is known, all
attempts for a really principled rationale are most problematic. According to archeological remains, it developed
historically only after musical theory of the Occident began to occupy itself with the investigation of consonances
and dissonances and their use in many-voiced writings.
This occurred only when contrary motions as an artistic
device and the usefulness of thirds and sixths as intervals
(in faux-bourdon) were recognized and, finally, after the
first really singable creations of polyphonic art compositions became available. Then precisely the change of intervals, regulated by artistic norms, was cultivated as a
special artistic device.

This appears as a product of the emancipation of polyvocality from completely opposite art practice now regarded as barbarous. As is known, the prohibition of parallels, which apparently was never objected to by any
artist in all its consequences, was accompanied by quite a
number of very perceptible barriers for melodic voice
motion. Beside the tonality of polyphony, in a narrower
sense, there gradually developed a condition the final result of which served the practical demands of chordal
harmony. As we have seen, through the entire Middle
Ages to the eighteenth century, it rested on the tonally
unstable foundation of the church modes. Out of the independence of several voices, the older writing for many

voices (especially the *motetus* of the thirteenth and fourteenth centuries) did not hesitate to supply them with
entirely different texts.[13] The practice was also justified of
permitting single voices to be written in several church
modes (which according to the intervals between the
different voices was, indeed, often directly unavoidable,
whenever chordal and harmonic unity was observed).
The extension of the church modes to twelve by Glarean
in the sixteenth century [14] by including the Ionian (on C)
and Aeolian (on A) modes which were used in other than
church music long before, implied the final renunciation
of the residues of old tetrachord tonality. The principles
of final and of half cadences of polyphonic music correspond even more clearly to the demand for chordal harmony which grew next to it and with it, even partly
against it, subject to peculiarities which were always especially retained in the Phrygian mode (the Hellenic
Dorian) and which had to be retained because of its
structure.

Inevitably the position of the dissonances was different
in contrapuntal polyphony from those in chordal harmony.
The appearance of theories dealing with the dissonances
marks the beginning of the special musical development
of the Occident. While the old strict (note against note)
polyphonic writing avoids direct dissonances, the oldest
theories of many-voiced writing, though permitting them,
refer them to the unaccentuated beats of the measure. In
the writing of several notes against one, this remained a
permanent feature of contrapuntalism while in chordal
harmony, the proper place of the dynamic dissonance is
precisely the accentuated part of the measure. In principle,
at least in strict polyphony, chords are only considered as
elements of the beauty of sonority. Unlike chordal har-

mony the dissonance is not the specifically dynamic element which gives birth to melodic progression but, by
contrast, is a product of voice progressions which are
strictly determined by their melodies. Thus, in principle,
it is always accidental and, where the originating chords
present a harmonic dissonance, it must always appear in
a sustained manner. This contrast of harmonic and polyphonic music is already rather clearly recognized in the
fifteenth century in the treatment of dissonance in the
Italian vernacular song, on the one hand, and in the ecclesiastical art of the Netherlands, on the other.

Harmonic-Homophonic Music

Harmonic-homophonic music as the third pure type
of polyvocality, is confronted by polyphony and strict
chordal harmony. It is called polyvocality only for technical reasons. It represents the subordination of the entire
tone setting under one voice carrying the melody, as its
harmonic accompaniment or supplement or interpretation
in all the most varied forms such relations can take. Primitive and preparatory stages of this type can be found
diffused in the most varied forms over the world. But they
were apparently nowhere so far developed as in the Occident as early as the fourteenth century (in Italy).[15] Only
since the beginning of the seventeenth century has it
been developed with full consciousness as an artistic style
in the music of Western civilization, again first in Italy,
particularly in the opera.

The primitive preparatory stages of polyvocality assume various forms which correspond to these pure types.
The accompaniment of a voice part can be found as vocal
and instrumental in unrationalized music systems. Some-

times, in quantitative terms, the accompanying voice is simply characterized by the fact that although it carries a melody of its own it is sung more softly. This occurs, for example, in the folk song in Iceland, where the accompanying voice proceeds with its own melody. Sometimes the accompanying voice is characterized by the fact that it appears to be qualitatively dependent on the voice which carries the melody in such manner that it circles round the latter in the form of passing tones or coloraturas. This occurs frequently in other music systems as, for example, in the Eastern-Asiatic (Chinese and Japanese).[16] It also appears as κροῦσις ὑπὸ τὴν ᾠδήν, if H. Riemann is right in his interpretation of the disputed concept, in old Hellenic music (as the only vestige of many-voiced writing known to this music.)[17] The instruments harmonize with the vocal part but insert coloraturas between the latter's sustained main tones (for which, according to Byzantine sources, evidently typical patterns existed). Or, beside the melodic motion one or more simultaneous accompanying tones are sustained in the form of bourdons.

In all these instances either the lower or upper vocal or instrumental voice can be the accompaniment. In vocal as well as instrumental polyvocality of this kind with more than two voices, the middle voice appears rather often as carrier of the melody (tenor, *cantus firmus* in the language of the Middle Ages). This is the case in Javanese gamelan music [18] where the vocal part recites the text, or in case of purely instrumental music, where the percussion instruments lead the *cantus firmus* in the middle voice. Upper voices of *musica figurata* nature appear next to it and a lower voice marks certain single tones according to its own rhythm. In Occidental art music during the Mid-

dle Ages it was taken for granted that the principal voice
(originally it was exclusively a motive from the Gregorian
chant) was the lower one above which the descant executed its melodic figurations. So exclusively was this the
case that when the reverse distribution of the melody in
the third and sixth songs, of the French and English so
important in music history, penetrated into art music it
was designated as faux-bourdon (false accompaniment),
a name it retained permanently.

The fact that the upper voice became the melodic vehicle was of far-reaching significance for the formation
of harmony. It was especially important for the position
of the bass as harmonic foundation. This was only a product of a long evolution in Occidental art music. The primitive bourdon was not yet a bass part in the sense that the
sustained tone should always lie in the lower voice. Von
Hornbostel cites the occurrence of a vocal bordon precisely in the upper voice for the music of a tribe of Sumatra (Kubu) [19] although it is the rule that the bourdon is of
instrumental nature and lies in the lower voice. Furthermore, the bourdon is by no means generally to be interpreted as a harmonic basis, like an organ point. Like any
primitive polyvocality, it is often to be interpreted only
as an aesthetic device used to achieve full sonority. It is
then without harmonic significance, having at least primarily rhythmic significance, particularly where it is produced by percussion instruments. Often, however, it has
a so-called indirect harmonic meaning, even in those cases
where it only appears as a drone bass produced by percussion instruments (gongs, tone sticks). In such cases
the percussion instrument does not supply only (or rather
not directly) the rhythm of the song, for it sometimes appears to be quite unconcerned in its own rhythm. The

singer assigned to the drone bass does not provide the rhythm but the support of the melody when that bass is missing. The varying distance to which he is assigned below the melody and the accompanying tone evidently serves as a basis for the melody in spite of its harmonic irrationality.

Finally the direct orientation of the principal tone of the song can frequently be determined according to the bordon (as with the North American Indians). The final cadence of the tone given by the percussion instrument is taken as the normal one by the Hindus and occasionally by other peoples. Then something similar to our *basso ostinato* can easily develop from the occurrence of a two-part bourdon (i.e., of instruments tuned in fifths and octaves). Such is known to Japanese (instrumental) gagaku music in which the koto (horizontal harp) takes over this role.[20] Where the sense for harmony is growing with the bordon, particularly the instrumental one, which is the lowest part, this evolution can be accelerated by the development of the instrumental bourdon into a kind of bass formation, accomplishing the formation of consonances from below.

This type of polyvocality subordinated to the upper voice is now confronted with the recently named "heterophony," as a preparatory stage of co-ordinating polyphony. It consists of a simultaneous performance of several voices in several melodic variants in which each of the several voices apparently goes its own way without concern for the others. In any case, the kinds of chords that appear are not consciously planned. This is usually found in connection with an instrumental accompaniment that serves as a basis. However, it also appears without instrumental accompaniment, even on most primitive levels of musical development.

In its most primitive form, heterophony, as with the Veddas who possess no instruments, appears as a confused singing of individuals who vary notes similar to those appearing in the solo. Such a plurality of individuals often conclude in the cadence either with the unison or with a consonant interval.

According to Wertheimer, heterophony appears as a product of singing together encouraged by the fact that melodic cadential tones become larger and (especially) more constant in time value than in the solo. Thus the entrance of other voices is regulated.[21] Beautiful examples of original and rather advanced peasant's heterophony in Russian folk songs have been phonographically recorded for the Petersburg academy by Mrs. E. Linjeff. As in all ancient folk music, the heterophonic development of the theme is improvised.[22] The several voices do not disturb each other either rhythmically or melodically only because of an established communal tradition. People of different villages cannot sing together in a many-voiced fashion. Moreover, unified organization of either homophonic-harmonic or contrapuntal vocal ensembles is absent.

Still, even in purely improvised folk heterophony and, even more so in heterophonic art forms, chords are observed in such a way that certain dissonances are avoided and certain kinds of chords sought. This first appears in the cadential tones of melodic sections which terminate either in unisons or consonances, especially the fifth, as in Japanese heterophony. Chinese heterophony developed as far as and essentially no farther than the level of the early medieval descant which consisted partly in a separation of voices from unison into alternating consonances and back to unison, partly in the establishment of an improvised coloring in the upper voice above the tenor, which was the main melody borrowed from the Gregorian chant.

Once the several voices were harmonically linked, the most radical harmonic form was one of strict parallel motion of consonant intervals. Such was the often cited primitive organum of the early Middle Ages. It is diffused rather widely over the world. Even Hucbald mentions it somewhat inaccurately in the tenth century.[23] Often it is the oldest form of classical many-voiced art music (allegedly also in Japan). Fourth and fifth parallels are predominant (among the Indonesians, Bantu tribes, and others). Considering the importance of these intervals for the tuning of instruments, the strict prohibition of fifth parallelism in the art music of contrapuntalism and in classical music is decidedly original.

Von Hornbostel mentions the occurrence in the Admiralty Islands of second parallels such as were also ascribed to the Langobards.[24] Here the most perfect consonances and the tonus produced by them as a residue were the preferred vehicle of the parallels. Chords of seconds which are said also to be found in the final cadences of Japanese gagaku music are not performed, at least in Japan, as a chord with simultaneously struck notes but as an arpeggio, according to the explanations of a Japanese musician reported by Stumpf.

In contrast to these cases as far as is known, till now real first parallels, such as the harmonic use of the third, seem to be found only in isolated instances. In choral songs in Togoland and Cameroun, perhaps due to European influence, alternations between major and minor thirds appear.[25] They can also be found as harp passages in one of the instrumental interludes of the Bantu, reported by Trilles. Until the present the third and (through its octave-wise duplication) the sixth as typical autonomous bases of polyphony appear with provable certainly only in northern Europe, especially England and France, the home countries of faux-bourdon and of the development of medieval polyvocality in general. The fact that the popular bicinium in Portugal should know third and sixth parallels beside fifths can be attributed to the influence of the development of sacred music.

The existence of polyvocality even on the basis of harmonic intervals of the whole-tone system of a musical composition does not by itself indicate the penetration of principles of harmonic tone construction. On the contrary, as noted in connection with von Hornbostel, melodicism may remain so completely untouched by it that it continues to use neutral thirds and similar irrational intervals. The tension between melodic and harmonic forces is already characteristic of primitive polyvocality. Hence no evolution toward harmonic music could have begun with the organum of the Occident, if other conditions, especially pure diatonicism as a basis of the tone system of art music, had not already existed.

Musical Notation as a Precondition of the Development of Harmonic-Homophonic Music

Evidently no uniform reply, either for the past or present, can be given to the question, Why did polyvocality appear in some parts of the world but not in others? Among factors which could have co-operated and allied themselves with chance occurrences no longer accessible to produce polyvocality the following stand out: (*1*) the different tempo, adequate for the use of instruments by themselves and in relation to the vocal part; (*2*) the sustained tones of the wind instruments in relation to the plucked ones of the strings; (*3*) in antiphonal singing the resounding or sustaining, found nearly everywhere, of the extended cadential tones of one voice during the entrance of the other; (*4*) the sonority of the repercussion tones of the harp at the arpeggio touch; (*5*) the polysonority of some ancient wind instruments with imperfect technical mastery; finally, (*6*) according to the circumstances, the simultaneous tone production while tuning instruments.

Another question arises: Why did polyphonic as well as harmonic-homophonic music and the modern tone system develop out of the widely diffused preconditions of polyvocality only in the Occident? Such preconditions were of at least equal intensity in other regions of the world and notably so in Hellenic antiquity and in Japan.

The specific conditions of musical development in the Occident involve, first of all, the invention of modern notation. A notation of our kind is of more fundamental importance for the existence of such music as we possess than is orthography for our linguistic art formations. This is perhaps true for all literary art with the possible exception of hieroglyphic literature and Chinese poetry for which, due to their artistic structure, the optical impression of the characters is integral to the full enjoyment of the poetic product. Still, any poetic product is nearly completely independent of the type and form of orthography. Disregarding the highest artistic performance of prose, perhaps on the height of the art of a Flaubert, or a Wilde, or of the analytic dialogues of an Ibsen, even today, in principle, the pure linguistic rhythmic work could be thought of as existing quite independently of orthography. A somewhat complicated modern work of music, on the other hand, is neither producible nor transmittable nor reproducible without the use of notation. It cannot exist anywhere and in any form at all, not even as an intimate possession of its creator.

Symbols of notes of some kind can be found on otherwise relatively primitive levels of musical development without correlation with rationalized melodicism. Although an object of theoretic treatment, modern Arabic music during the long period since the Mongolian attacks has gradually lost its old notational system and is now entirely without it. The Hellenes were consciously proud of their attribute as a nation with a musical notation.

Note symbols were quite indispensable for instrumental accompaniment as soon as it participated in more complicated pieces and not simply in unison with the vocal part. The technical formation of the older note symbols is without interest here. Even in Chinese music it is still extremely primitive. The art music systems of peoples with writing occasionally use numbers, but commonly letters serve for tone designation. This is also true for the Hellenes, where vocal and the older instrumental symbols stand for the same tone independently of each other. In Byzantine terminology the designation of the same melodic motion is different for song and instrument. The note symbols are unambiguously transmitted by the Alypic tables, a product of the period of the Emperors.[26] The very fact that such tables were kept indicates the practical complexity of the system.

The designations are especially detailed for the pykna of chromaticism and enharmonicism. As notes they would

have caused difficulties to the performer of any of the
more complicated pieces. Even a simple score would be
unthinkable by means of them. Rather, in practical musical performances, at least in the danced course songs, the
coryphaeus indicated the motion of the melos with his
hand as well as the rhythm with his foot. The cheironomy
was taken as an integral part of orchestrics and was also
practised in form of rhythmic gymnastics separately and
independently of the dance proper.

The development of letter designation, which in the
Western world occurs rather late, namely in the tenth century, appears, after some fluctuations to have taken the
letter *a* to designate the very tone which even today cor-
responds to it. This indicates at least one thing, that at
the time of their origin the church modes did not mean
anything, for otherwise, doubtlessly the letters would
have had to take the tetrachord system into consideration
in the same manner as with the Hellenes.

Letter designation did not play a lasting role in Occidental musical practice and it has finally disappeared
except in regions with weak development of many-voiced
writing, such as Germany. In the classical areas of many-
voiced writing the solmisation system with its hexachords
starting from G, C, and F served for the practice of the
diatonic scale since Guido's time and permitted the development of a gesture language by transferring the hexachord intervals to the fingers of the hand. This also occurs
in India.

Neumes first known in the Orient and later in Byzantine
church music were used for the benefit of singers. The
neumes represent a transference of cheironomic motions
into written symbols: shorthand symbols for groups of
melodic tone steps and singing modes. The transcription

of them has not been entirely successful despite the works of O. Fleischer, H. Riemann, J. B. Thibaut, von Riesemann, and others.[27] They neither indicate absolute pitch nor the time value of the single note, but only, as obviously as possible, the tone steps and singing modes to be performed within a single group of symbols (i.e., the glissando). Yet, as indicated by continuous controversies and varied interpretations by individual magisters of monastic choruses, even the tone steps and singing modes were not really given in an exact way.

In particular the neumes did not differentiate between whole and semitone steps. This circumstance favored flexibility of official musical patterns with respect to the musical needs of ordinary practice and favored the penetration of popular tonal traditions into musical development. As early as the ninth century, because of this unorderliness, the improvement of a notation had become an object of eager speculation by monastic musical scholars. Such speculations were carried on in the North (Hucbald) as well as in the South (the manuscript of Kircher of the Cloister S. Salvatore near Messina).[28] Moreover, the acceptance of polyvocality in the monastic chant and thus also under the materials of theory doubtless intensified the incentive for the creation of tone symbols easily read and comprehended. This is especially demonstrated in kind by Hucbald's attempts. However, the first important step, inserting the neumes into a system of staff lines, was not developed in the interest of polyvocality but to reduce melodic ambiguity of sign reading in singing. This is clearly indicated by Guido d'Arezzo's own appraisal of his invention (or rather, of his consistent use of the device of two-colored lines to designate the position of F and C, which had already been previously applied by monks).

The substitution of neumes which symbolized not only tones and intervals but also ways of performance and which were thus first taken over unchanged into the system of staff lines by simple dots and by squares and oblong note symbols, paralleled the second decisive developmental step. This was the introduction of the time value indications together with the tone designation, the work of the so-called mensural notation which occurred since the beginning of the twelfth century. It was primarily the work of music theoreticians, mainly monks close to the musical practice of Notre Dame and the Cathedral of Cologne. The details of this development so fundamental for Occidental music are out of place here. They are analyzed in the work of J. Wolf.[29] It is necessary for us only to note that they were the necessary consequence of certain very specific polyphonic problems in the area of rhythm. So far as it is important for development of rhythm, it will be examined later.

The decisive element for polyvocality was the fact that the establishment of the relative time value of the tone symbols and the fixed pattern of measure division now permitted the unambiguous determination of the relations of progression of the individual voices in a manner easily surveyed. Thus a truly polyvocal composition was made possible. In itself, this was by no means established by the development of artistically organized polyvocality. Even when the many-voiced accompaniment of a basic melody, considered as the tenor, had developed into a measured art, the composing of descants still remained largely improvisation (*contrapunctus a mente*), perhaps in the same way as the later playing of the *basso continuo*. Even up

to the end of the seventeenth century, as in the contract
quoted by Caffi, of the band of San Marco in Venice in
1681,[30] the bands often listed a special *contrapunto* with
the singers of the *canto fermo*. The papal band required
of all applicants the ability to improvise counterpoint.[31]
As, later, the player of the thorough bass, the contra-
puntalist had to stand on the summit of the musical art
education of his time in order to find the correct counterpoint, *super librum,* i.e., the available part of the singer
of the *cantus firmus*. The society of descant singers of the
papal group of Rome praised at the beginning of the
thirteenth century, was, in principle, of the same character.

However, first of all, mensural notation permitted the
planning of many-voiced art compositions. Also the great
prestige of the Flemish school of musical development of
the period from 1350 to 1550,[32] though overestimated in
his time due to the brilliant prize-winning essay of Kiesewetter,[33] rested quite essentially on the fact, so far as external circumstances played a role, that they brought
planned written compositions to the center of ecclesiastical
music. Moreover, the papal band, precisely after its return
from Avignon, was nearly exclusively dominated by them.

Only the elevation of many-voiced music under notational art created the composer proper and guaranteed the
polyphonic creations of the Western world, in contrast to
those of all other peoples, permanence, aftereffect, and
continuing development.

6. RATIONALIZATION OF THE TONE

SYSTEM AND TEMPERAMENT

The Western Development toward Strict Diatonicism

WITH a basis of rational notation it is obvious that polyvocality provided powerful support to the harmonic rationalization of the tone system. This was initially felt in the pressure toward strict diatonicism.

According to the best authorities (P. Wagner and Gevaert)[1] the Gregorian chant and its direct derivatives do not seem to contain any diatonic tones even after Carolingian times. One manuscript suggests that an occasional antique enharmonic splitting of semitones occurs, as in Byzantine music. In the *analysis organica* Byzantine theory was familiar with the enharmonic intervals on the string instruments for a descending tone series. Since they were most difficult, they were considered as the highest level of harmony.[2] Equivalent practice quickly vanished in the Occident around the tenth and eleventh centuries. From that time, at least in theory, diatonicism began to monopolize thinking.

Reaction against Pure Diatonicism

The implications of the supremacy of one particular tonality should not be misunderstood here nor for any musical system not conditioned harmonically. In Eastern-Asiatic, particularly Japanese music, where the semitone is much enjoyed, also in Chinese as well as in Occidental music in the early Middle Ages, the progression laid down in the tone symbols is often merely the skeleton or frame for the real performance.

Moreover, improvised ornaments of many kinds, especially prolonged tones in final cadences, were permissible spontaneous tasks of the singer. The singers and even more, the magistri of the greater bands assumed the right to balance melodic harshness by chromatic tone alterations. The older neume notation, common to Orient and Occident, furthered this tendency by its failure to differentiate univocally between whole and semitone. In Byzantine notation there are ἄφωνα tones which although sung were not counted (rhythmically). In the Western world the extent to which melodious alterations should be included in the notation was continually discussed. Guido d'Arezzo designed his notational innovations precisely to remedy the arbitrariness possible here. However it persisted in the face of Guido's rigid diatonicism.

The fact that the great majority of all tone alterations are not fixed in writing presents a major difficulty for deciphering archeological music fragments. The restraints fixed by sacred music theory and practice on alterations did not prevent popular influence of church songs. The great quantity of old folk songs appears to have been deeply influenced by the diatonicism of the church modes. The church modes could hardly have acquired this influence without the flexibility noted above. With increasing response to expressive needs the effects of this elasticity became ever more extensive. After five hundred years several chorales, the purely diatonic intonation of which is known since the fifteenth century, are, as provable by details, being sung today with chromatic tone alterations. The latter is stretched until it is almost unrecognizable and has become a permanent official possession.

More important than alterations of the individual song, the church modes themselves had to yield to the continuing permanent acceptance of musical elements originally foreign to them. This led to the schism which shattered the musical supremacy of the church. The third (in fauxbourdon, which probably at the time was taken over officially by the church) and then regular chromaticism organized harmonically were accepted.

This further chromaticism, though originating as a revolt against pure diatonicism, developed internally on the basis of the diatonic church modes, from the beginning creating tone material which was to be interpreted in harmonic fashion. It grew precisely within the musical system which already possessed a rationally regulated polyvocality, presented in a harmonically rational notation.

Quite apart from Hellenic enharmonicism in tonally less developed music systems which lack polyvocal writing or its rationalization, not only new 3/4 and 5/4 tones but even completely irrational intervals are joined to the older intervals as a product of the drive for melodic expressiveness. Basque music, the age of which is uncertain, not only inserts semitones in the diatonic basic scale, but does so, apparently arbitrarily.[3] Thus to our musical sensibilities it not only changes rapidly from major to minor but also creates entire formation without tonality, although it apparently at a change of key obeys certain rules (leading tone) which determine the principal tones. From the tenth to the thirteenth century, the Arabian scale experienced a twofold enrichment with increasingly irrational intervals.

As soon as the strong grip of the typical tone formula is loosened and the virtuoso or professional artist trained for virtuoso-like performances becomes the carrier of musical development, there is no firm barrier against the extensive growth of tonal elements arising through new expressive needs. Perhaps it is characteristic that, so far as I can see, among the songs of the Ewe Negroes published by Fr. Witte, those which are farthest away from a restless tonal rationalizability (especially in the final cadence and half cadence tones) are two very fast epics performed by master singers in which an irrational, chromatically sharpened tone sequence (not in individual irrational tones) appears as a forerunner of the transition into another key. By contrast, simpler songs are poorer in alterations (and apparently are more apathetic).[4]

We can perceive several phenomena which dissolve tonality in our own musical development. This has been testified to as well for completely heterogeneous conditions for the evident reason that the use of entirely irrational expressive devices can often be understood as the product of a baroque and affected aesthetic manner, sort of an intellectualistic epicureanism. Under otherwise relatively primitive conditions this most easily arises in the circles of a guild of learned musicians who monopolize court music. The analogy can be drawn to the Nordic court scaldic art with its linguistic creations which defy any taste.

For this same reason not all irrational intervals are a product of primitive musical development. A music which is not harmonically rationalized is much freer in its motions. Also an ear which, unlike ours, does not, by training unconsciously interpret each interval born out of pure melodic and expressive needs in harmonic terms, is not restricted to the enjoyment of intervals which it can classify harmonically. Thus it is understandable that music systems which once permanently appropriate an irrational interval are particularly inclined to accept others.

All Oriental music contains the irrational third, which probably originated from the old bagpipe, a primitive instrument known to all cattle breeders and Bedouins. It is evidently permanently attached to the peculiar ethos of this very irrationality.[5] Thus the music reformers were repeatedly lucky with the creation of irrational thirds. The diffusion of Arabic music over the whole of Asia Minor restricted any development toward harmony or, even, pure diatonicism. Only the Jewish synagogue song was unaffected.[6] Apparently it was retained in a form which is very closely related to the church modes which, indeed, makes somewhat plausible the often maintained relationship of old Christian with Jewish psalmody and hymnology.

Rationalization by Means of an Arbitrary Equalization of Tones

The flexibility of the melodicism of nonharmonically conditioned music provided space for rationalization by an arbitrary equalization of those tones lacking in perfect tuning. Such tones always result from the unsymmetrical division of the octave and from the dissociation of different interval circles.

This kind of rationalization could and did occur partly in a completely extramusical manner. Historically the rationalization of tones normally starts from the instruments: the length of the bamboo flute in China, the tension of the strings of the kithara in Hellas, the length of the strings of the lute in Arabia, of the monochord in Occidental cloisters. In their respective areas these instruments served for the physical measurement of consonances. In these cases the instruments were tuned from heard tones and only used for the more exact determination and settlement of consonance intervals. They were employed in the service of previously fixed tonal requirements.

However, the reverse was possible and did occur. Certain ancient Central American wind instruments show a hole distribution in accordance with purely symmetrical ornamental requirements to which the played tones conformed.[7] This is neither unusual nor characteristic only of barbarian music.

The Arabian music system, the external fate of which was previously discussed, was a true drill ground for experimentation of the theorists. They continued the Hellenistic speculations, under Hellenistic and Persian influence, concerning purely mathematical intervals. This doubtless occurred remote from actual musical practice. To the present the intervals of Arabic music system are determined by experiments of the Persians. In a purely mechanical division of space they inserted between the frets for the forefinger (salaba) and the ring finger (bincir) a completely irrational third (assessed as 68/81 by the theorists) for the middle finger (wosta-wusta). Then

Zalzal by another mechanically equal separation of the space between the Persian wosta and the bincir inserted another irrational third (assessed at 22/27) which was closer to the harmonic third. It holds its ground today.[8]

This was neither the only nor first insertion of this kind. Other instruments were subject to even more radical experiments. The tanbur from Bagdad [9] with two strings, whose intervals were already thought to be pagan, i.e., pre-Islamic, by Al Farabi [10] is certainly a primitively divided instrument, for it gained intervals by a mechanically equal division of one eighth of a string in five equal parts, thereby distance of 39/40 upward to 6/8 resulted. Evidently the rabab (rebab) with two strings had to serve experimentally for the division of the octave by an interval between a fourth and a fifth in two parts really equal in terms of distance. But the string represents the ambitus of a peculiar tritone interval which arises when the large third is augmented by a whole tone (the same happens in Arabic assessment, if the ditone is increased by a minor whole tone). If the intervals were harmonically assessed this resulted either in the harmonic augmented fourth (f-sharp) or, and this was always the case in Arabic music which calculated downwards, in the harmonically diminished lower fifth of the upper octave (g-flat) equals 32/45, which comes rather close to the second power 1024/2025 indeed to $\sqrt[2]{2}$ of the algebraic and equal divisions of the octave interval. The intervals of the strings contained the second, the harmonically minor third, and the ditone. Since the strings were separated from each other by a minor third when tuned the scale contained the tonic, the second, the harmonically minor third, the ditone, the fourth, a somewhat too small interval standing close to the algebraic half of the octave, and two smaller thirds (625/1206 [sic] = 1/2.08) harmonic octave), a fifth being too high by the pythagorean comma, and finally the pythagorean sixth. Al Farabi also rejects this scale, which evidently originated from intervallic rationalization within the octave, but which certainly was not primitive. Already in the musical practice of Al Farabi's time, it is reported that the intervals of the tanbur of Bagdad were not retained but struck in a deviating manner, doubtless in correspondence with the fret intervals.

By contrast the octave division could not have remained without influence on the rabab. Probably it was under this influence that the fifth, the fundamental harmonic Arabian and Indian interval, raised the tritone to the status of an important interval. In contrast to the almost completely irrational intervals of the tanbur, this interval is easily rationalized.

Moreover, Zalzal's third, which was created arbitrarily, still appears in the scales of Meschaka. It was based on the old Oriental neutral bagpipe third. Chinese music, indeed, shows that intervals created mechanically and arbitrarily without musical basis can be permanently embodied in a musical system. The main instrument of the Eastern-Asiatic orchestra, the king (percussion instrument or harmonized stone or metal plate) had very obviously not been determined in its tuning by musical consideration, but by requirements of mechanical symmetry.[11] It is evident how strongly such antimusical arbitrariness could alter musical sensitivity and divert it from an understanding of harmonic relations. Without doubt such antimusical considerations profoundly influence the musical development of some peoples and are probably responsible for the stalemate of Eastern-Asiatic music on a "tonal" level which was otherwise only peculiar to primitive peoples.

Rationalization from within the Tone System: Temperament

Extra-musical rationalistic alteration of the tone system contrasts sharply with rationalization from within, in terms of the specific character of melodicism and in the interest in the symmetry and comparability of tone distances. We are familiar with attempts to find a common distance denominator for the intervals of the octave from Chinese, Indian, and Hellenic experiments. Since all attempts at rationalization do not balance evenly on the basis of the harmonic, thus resulting in the distance-wise unequal division of the octave, at all times and precisely in melodic music systems the obvious attempt was made to reach rational results in a special way, by temperament.

In the broadest meaning, any tone scale is tempered when the distance principle is applied in such a manner that the purity of the intervals is relativized for the purpose of equalization of contradictions between different interval circles, reducing distances to only approximate tone purity.

In the most extreme pure type, one interval, naturally the octave which in turn does not tolerate any merely relative tone purity, is taken as a basis for the scale and simply divided into equally large tone distances. In Siamese music it is divided into seven,[12] in Javanese music [13] it is divided into five, to that single tone steps become $\sqrt[7]{1/2}$ and $\sqrt[5]{1/2}$ respectively. In such extreme cases one cannot speak of a temperament of harmonic intervals, the relativization of their purity, but of scale rationalization as

presented on truly musical, yet entirely extraharmonic
bases (with the exception of the octave itself). In the
case of the Siamese it seems probable that the historical
starting point was the division into fifths and fourths, for
according to Stumpf's investigations [14] precisely these im-
perfections, which also according to our feelings are most
objectionable, were avoided as far as possible. There were
intervals lying close to the fourth. This was followed
(possibly passing through pentatonicism) by the present
rationalization which was founded solely on extraordi-
narily acute sensitivity by the Siamese for intervals, a
sensitivity surpassing the achievement of the best European piano-tuners (according to Stumpf's investigations).
As the phenomenon of physical distinctiveness of consonances in terms of numbers always encouraged the
mythological interpretation of tones in numerical terms, it
is probable that the holiness of the numbers 5 and (particularly) 7 influenced the type of division.[15] Of course,
practically, temperament for purely melodic music is
essentially a device to accomplish the transposition of
melodies into any pitch without retuning the instruments.

Temperament is very close to music oriented primarily
toward intervallic melodicism. In Hellenic antiquity, Aristoxenus was its advocate in his function as a tone psy-
chologist. He rejected the idea of rationalization by
instruments and the dominance of purely virtuoso instrumental music. He thought that the ear alone should
decide upon the worth or worthlessness of melodic intervals. In the near and far East, even the experimentation with quarter tones and other small intervals as
atomic units of the tone system suggested the idea of a
temperament. In reality temperament was not carried out
anywhere except in the cases mentioned which belong to

the topic of extramusical violence. In their deviations from the official intervals Japanese singers seem to glide as often to the side of perfect as to the side of tempered tuning.

Despite its obvious affinities with melodic music, the principle of temperament did not find its most important home ground in melodic music. For temperament was also the last word in our chordal and harmonic development. Inasmuch as physical tone rationalization always meets somewhere with the fatal comma and pure tuning, especially since it only presents a relative optimum of an ensemble of fifths, fourths, and thirds, since the sixteenth century a partial temperament already prevailed for the special Occidental instruments, the keyboard instruments.

At the time the range of these instruments was little more than that of the voice. The main function of the keyboard instruments was vocal accompaniment. Thus tuning depended on the balance with the four middle fifths of our present piano (C-e′) and the purity of the interval of the third, which at that time penetrated the music from within and which was the center of interest.

The means for obtaining the balance varied. According to Schlick's suggestion the "unequally floating" temperament, by tempering of the fifth, should tune in a perfect way that e which appears as the fourth fifth in the circle of fifths starting from C. The "middle tone" temperament was more practical. Schlick's suggestion had the defect of all "unequally floating" temperaments. Altering the fifths brought fourths into existence. The fifths so important to the music of the time are the notorious "wolf" of the organ-builders, through whose hands all problems of tuning passed.

The increase in the range of organ and piano, the

striving after its complete exploitation in purely instrumental music, in contrast with the difficulty of using
pianos with some thirty to fifty keys on the octave in
piano tempo were forces on temperament. In principle
no upper limit can be assigned to the number of keys to
the octave if one wants to construe pure intervals for
each circle. The requirements of freer transposition and
especially of freer movements lead forcefully toward
equal floating temperament: the division of the octave
into twelve equal distances of equivalent semitones $\sqrt[12]{1/2}$.
The result is twelve fifths with seven octaves, the aboli-
tion of enharmonic dieses, which finally, after a hard
struggle, won for all instruments with fixed keys. This was
brought about theoretically under the influence of
Rameau, practically through the effect of J. S. Bach's
"well-tempered piano" and the school works of his son.[16]

However, for chord music temperament presupposed
the free progression of chords which without it had to be
triturated continuously by the coexistence of various sevenths, completely perfect and completely imperfect fifths,
thirds, and sixths. But through the so-called "enharmonic
exchange" it positively offered entirely new and highly
productive possibilities for modulation, namely putting
another sense of a chord or tone upon a chord relation in
which it is written into another. This is a specifically
modern modulatory device, at least so far as employed
consciously. By contrast the meaning of the polyphonic
music of the past was very frequently related to the tonality of the church modes.

Though it has been occasionally maintained, it cannot
be ascertained for certain that the Hellenes construed and
used their enharmonic partial tones for similar reasons.
This supposition is contrary to the character of these tones

which originated through the splitting up of tone distances. Their modulatory devices were quite different, even though the pyknon (as in the Apollo hymn) occasionally played a role in the transition to the synemmenon which, however, would have been a purely melodic relation and cannot be compared to the enharmonic relations of the present. This is similar to the purely melodic function of an irrational tone series which can, apparently, be found in Negro music systems. The principal bearer of the enharmonic exchange in chord music was obviously the diminished seventh chord (for instance, f-sharp, a, c, e-flat) proper to any scale on the major seventh of the minor keys (for instance, g-minor) with resolutions into eight different keys always according to the enharmonic interpretation of its intervals. The whole of modern chordal harmonic music is unthinkable without temperament and its consequences. Only temperament brought it to full freedom.

Peculiarities of Occidental Temperament

The peculiarity of modern temperament is found in the fact that the practical execution of the principle of distance is operative on our keyboard instruments as a temperament of tones gained harmonically. It is not like the so-called temperament in the tone systems of the Siamese and Javanese, merely a creation of a real distance scale rather than a harmonic scale. Beside the distance-wise measurement of the intervals is the choral and harmonic interpretation of intervals. Theoretically it dominates the orthography of notation.

Without this quality modern music would neither have been technically nor meaningfully possible. Its meaning rests on the fact that tone successions are not treated as an indifferent series of semitones. Despite all orthographic liberties taken even by the masters, it clings fast to the signation of the tones according to their harmonic meaning. Obviously the fact cannot be changed that even our notation, corresponding to its historical origins, is limited in the exactitude of its harmonic tone designation and reproduces, above all, the enharmonic but not the chromatic precision of the tones. For example, notation ignores the fact that the chord d–f–a according to the provenience of the tones is a genuine minor triad or a musically irrational combination of the pythagorean and minor third. But, even so, the significance of our type of notation is great enough. Although explainable only from a historical viewpoint it is not merely an antiquarian reminiscence.

Our musical sensitivity also is dominated by the interpretation of the tones according to their harmonic provenience. We feel, even "hear," in a different fashion the tones which can be identified enharmonically on the instruments according to their chordal significance. Even the most modern developments of music, which are practically moving in many ways toward a destruction of tonality, show this influence. These modern movements which are at least in part the products of the characteristic, intellectualized romantic turn of our search for the effects of the "interesting," cannot get rid of some residual relations to these fundaments, even if in the form of developing contrasts to them.

There is no doubt that the distance principle which is akin to harmony and which is the basis of the subdivision of the intervals of our keyboard instruments, has an extensively dulling effect upon the delicacy of listening ability. The frequent use of enharmonic exchanges in modern music has a parallel effect on our harmonic feeling.

Though tonal ratio is hardly able to capture the living motion of musically expressive devices, it is, nevertheless, everywhere effective, be it ever so indirectly and behind the scenes, as a form-giving principle. It is particularly strong in music like ours where it has been made the conscious fundament of the tone system. Theoretically the modern tone system is not understandable without its effects. Nor has its influence fallen exclusively upon what already existed in musical practice. To be sure, repeatedly it has tended to place our music in persistent dragging chains.

Certainly modern chordal harmony belonged to practical music long before Rameau and the encylopedists provided it with a theoretic basis (still somewhat imperfect).[17] The fact that this occurred was productive of effects in musical practice quite in the same manner as the rationalization efforts of the medieval theorists for the development of polyvocality which existed before their assistance. The relations between tonal ratio and musical life belong to the historically most important and varying situations of tension in music.

7. TECHNICAL, ECONOMIC, AND SOCIAL INTERRELATIONS BETWEEN MODERN MUSIC AND ITS INSTRUMENTS

Origins of the Strings

OUR string instruments which are akin to those of antique culture and known in a primitive form to the Chinese and other music systems, represent the convergence of two different species of instruments. On the one hand, they are descendants of the violin-like string instruments native to the Orient and the tropical regions, provided with a resonant body made of one piece (originally the shell of the tortoise with skin stretched above it).

The lyre known from Otfried in the eighth century which consisted of one, later three and more strings, belonged to these instruments as did the rubeba (rebek) imported from the Orient during the crusades and used extensively in the eleventh, twelfth, and thirteenth centuries. This instrument was well adapted to traditional music. It was able to produce the diatonic church modes including the b-moll (b-flat). However, it was not properly of progressive nature. Neither the resonance nor the cantilena was ready to be developed beyond narrow limits.

These instruments were confronted by string instruments with a resonant body built as a composite and provided with special string parts (frets). These made possible the formation of the resonant body necessary for an unhindered manipulation of the bow and its optimal equipment with the modern resonance bearers (bridge, sound post). For the effectiveness of string instruments shaping of the resonant body is decisive. A string merely firmly strung without a vibrating body does not produce a musically useful tone.

The creation of resonant bodies is a purely Occidental invention, the specific motive for which can no longer be ascertained. It seems to be related to the fact that the handling of wood in the form of boards and all finer carpenter's and wooden inlay work is much more typical of Nordic peoples than those of the Orient.

The Hellenic plucked string instruments with their resonant bodies, which in comparison with those of the Orient, were already built artistically, were subject, thus, after their migration north, to very early further improvement precisely in those respects. The first instruments with raised borders were still of rather primitive kind. The one stringed *trumscheit* which probably originated from the monochord had a resonant board body with transmission of the vibrations by means of a sound post and produced by means of simple technical devices a strong, trumpet-like increased sound.[1] Tone production did not take place mechanically but through fingered manipulation. Only experts could produce other than first harmonics. Without doubt because of its very tonal limitations, the instrument re-enforced modern tone feeling. The wheel lyre (organistrum), a keyboard instrument with raised borders, produced the diatonic scale, but it also possessed bourdon strings tuned in fifths and fourths. Like the trumscheit it was domesticated in the monasteries of the early Middle Ages.

Whether wheel lyres were originally in the hands of jongleurs cannot be established, but they were never the instruments of noble amateurs. Next to the lyre among the instruments important to the jongleurs later belongs the Germanic and Slavic fiddle, which is already found in the ninth century.[2] It was the instrument of the Nibelungen heroes. For the first time on it, the neck was formed as a separate part supplying the sturdiness needed for its use in a modern fashion.

The fiddle (called by Hieronymus of Moravia "vielle") originally had two unison strings (for the third accompaniment) and bourdon strings or none of this kind depending on whether artistic or popular music was to be performed.[3] From the fourteenth to the eighteenth century it also had frets. As long as the requirements of orchestra music did not take possession and transform it, the instrument had increasing harmonic importance. Because of its technique and hardiness it became the bearer of folk tunes.

Evolution of String Instruments under the Influence of the Bards

Social organizational factors contributed additional forces to the evolution of the strings. The Gaelic crwth, important as the instrument of the bards, was originally plucked and later played.[4] The rules for playing it were subject to regulation through congresses of bards (as, for example, the Congress of 1176).[5] It is the first of many string instruments with a bridge and holes through which the hand may be passed. Subjected to continuous technical improvement, it became harmonically useful after the addition of the bourdon strings. The crwth is today considered to be the ancestor of the fiddle with raised borders.

Professional organization secured the musical influence of the bards. This in turn was a basic factor in the continuous improvement and typification of their instruments. These instruments were indispensable for the advancement of music.

Furthermore, technical improvements in the construction of string instruments was connected, toward the end of the Middle Ages, with the musical guild organizations of instrumentalists which in the Sachsenspiegel were still treated as having no legal rights. This guild organization appeared in the thirteenth century, providing a fixed market for the manufactured instruments, helping standardize their types.

Still other social factors are represented in the gradual acceptance of instrumentalists beside the singers in the bands of the hierarchy, of princes, and of communities. Established instrumental roles became the rule only in the sixteenth century. This gave to the production of instruments an even more productive economic foundation. Since the fifteenth century in close connection with humanistic music theorists, the attempt was made to provide instruments ready to be played in orchestras. The separation of the high and low viols was executed at least with the French *ménétriers* of the fourteenth century.

The Great Instrument-Makers and the Modern Orchestra

The numerous species of viols still found in the seventeenth and eighteenth centuries with very different, often very numerous stringing, recalling the rapid increase of strings on the Hellenic kithara, were a product of uninterrupted experimentation especially in the sixteenth century. It was also encouraged by the individually varied traditional practices and pretensions of the leading orchestras. These numerous types of viols vanished in the eighteenth century in favor of the three modern string instruments: the violin, viola, and cello. The superiority of these instruments was unambiguously demonstrated by violin virtuosity first appearing in full bloom since Corelli, and through development of the modern orchestra.

The violin, viola, and cello became the instruments for a special modern organization of chamber music, the string quartet as it was definitely established by Joseph Haydn. They constitute the kernel of the modern orchestra. They are a product of persistent experiments of the manufacturers of instruments from Brescia and Cremona.

The gap between the performance capacity of these instruments, which were in no way improved since the beginning of the eighteenth century, and their predecessors is very striking. Speaking with some exaggeration, the string instruments of the Middle Ages did not permit the legato playing which in our view is specific to them, although the ligatures of old mensural notation permit us to conclude they existed. The sustaining of tones, increasing or decreasing volume, melodious playing of fast passages, and all the specific qualities which we expect to be executed by the violin were still rendered only with difficulty until the sixteenth century. They were nearly impossible quite apart from the fact that the changes of hand position required today for the domination of the tone space of string instruments were almost excluded by the type of construction. Considering the quality of the family of instruments it is not surprising that the division of the neck through frets, thus mechanical tone production, prevailed. Virdung, therefore, still calls the hand fiddle together with the more primitive string instruments useless.[6]

In connection with the demand of court orchestras the ascension of string instruments to their perfection began in the sixteenth century. The ever-present desire for expressive sonorous beauty, for a singing tone, and elegance of the instrument itself were the driving forces in Italy of the orchestras and the instrument-makers. Even before the transfer of technical supremacy in violin construction to Brescia and Cremona, one notes in the sixteenth century, gradual approximations of various parts of the instrument (especially of the form of the bridge and the sound holes) toward its final form.

What such technical development offered in possibilities, once perfection was achieved, far surpassed what had been demanded. The performance capacity of the Amati instruments was not really exploited for many decades. In the same way as the single violin, following an ineradicable conviction, first had to be "played in" and had to wait a generation before it could reach the full height of its rendition potential, so the adaptation and introduction also as compared with other instruments occurred only very slowly. Ruhlmann's supposition that modern string instruments originate in a unique, unanticipated accident goes too far. However, it remains true that the tonal potential made available by the construction of the instrument was not immediately exploited. Its availability as a special solo instrument of virtuosi could not have been guessed beforehand by the builders.

It is to be assumed that the concern of the Amati, Guarneri, and Stradivari were turned essentially toward achieving sensuous beauty and only then sturdiness in the interest of the greatest possible freedom of movement by the player. The restriction to four strings, the omission of frets, therewith mechanical tone production, and the final fixing of all single parts of the resonant body and of the systems of conducting the vibration were aesthetic consequences. Other qualities devolved upon them in the form of "secondary products" as much unwilled as the atmospheric effects of Gothic inner rooms was initially. These were involuntary consequences of purely constructive innovations.

In any case the production of the great violin-builders lacked a rational foundation such as can be clearly recognized with organ, the piano and its predecessors, as well as the wind instruments. The crwth was improved on grounds belonging to the guild. The string instruments were developed on the basis of purely empirical knowledge gained gradually in time as to the most useful shape of the top, the sound holes, the bridge and its perforation, the core, the post, the raised borders, the best qualities of wood and probably also varnish. This resulted in those achievements which today, perhaps because of the disappearance of the balsam fir, can no longer be completely imitated.

Considering their technical construction, instruments created in such manner did not as such consist of a device to promote harmonic music. On the contrary, the lack of the bridge of the older instruments facilitated their use in bringing forth chords and the bourdon strings served as the harmonic support of the melody. This was omitted in the modern instruments which, on the contrary, seemed designed as vehicles of melodic effects. Precisely this was welcome to the music of the Renaissance, governed as it was by dramatic interests.[7]

Social Ranking of the Instruments

The new instruments were soon employed in the orchestra of the operas (according to customary suppositions, first employed in modern fashion in *Orfeo* by Monteverdi). We do not initially hear anything of their use as solo instruments. This is due to the traditional social ranking of the instruments.

Since the lute was a court instrument, the lutenist was inside the pale of society. His salary in the orchestra of Queen Elizabeth was three times as much as that of the violinist, five times as much as that of the bagpipe-player. The organist was considered to be a complete artist.

Only by great efforts did the violinists first manage to gain recognition and only after this (especially through Corelli) did an extensive literature for string instruments begin to develop.

As the orchestra of the Middle Ages and Renaissance was built around the wind instruments, orchestra music today is as unthinkable without the violins. The exception is found in military music, the old natural home of wind instruments. The modern strings, precisely as used in orchestras, are indoor instruments which do not produce their full effect even in rooms surpassing a certain moder-

ate size—to be sure, a smaller size than is ordinarily used
today for chamber music.

The Keyboard Instruments: The Organ

To an even greater degree than the strings, indoor
character is important for the modern keyboard instruments.

The organ consists of a combination of the panpipes
with the principle of the bagpipe.[8] It was supposedly constructed by Archimedes. It was known in any case in the
second century B.C.[9] In the time of the Romans the organ
was a court, theatre, and festival instrument. It was particularly important as a festival instrument in Byzantium.

The antique water organ extolled by Tertullian, to be
sure without any technical comprehension, could not have
pentrated into our latitudes because of the freezing of
the water. Perhaps even before the use of water regulation, in any case since the fourth century (obelisk of
Theodosius in Constantinople) the pneumatic organ appeared. It came to the Occident from the Byzantine em-
pire. In Carolingian times it was still essentially a court
music machine. Louis the Pious did not put the organ he
received as a gift into the cathedral, but into the palace
in Aachen.

Where the organ penetrated into the monasteries it
became representative of all technical musical rationalization within the church. Also important, it was used for
musical instruction. The regular ecclesiastical use of the
organ is documented since the tenth century in connection
with festivals.

In the Occident from the beginning the organ underwent continuous uninterrupted technical improvement.

Around 1200 it had reached the range of three octaves. Since the thirteenth century, theoretic treatises were written about it. Since the fourteenth century its use in the large cathedrals has been universal. In the fourteenth century it became an instrument really capable of melodic performances, after the windchest had obtained its first rational form in the so-called *Springlade* for which at the end of the sixteenth century the *Schleiflade* was substituted.

In the early Middle Ages the organ was at best just able to play the *cantus firmus*. Planful mixtures were still unknown and unnecessary, for congregational singing did not exist and knowledge of the *cantus firmus* was not required. From the eleventh to the thirteenth century tones were formed by pulling out the keys, with up to forty pipes to a key in the oldest organs which are described in detail. A separation of tones as was later produced by the boards of the windchest was still impossible. For musical performance as such, compared with the pulled keys, the *Orgelschlagen,* beating with fists on the pressure keys, sometimes over a decimeter broad, was an advance, though inconstancy of the wind supply even then still strongly detracted from the perfection of its temperament.

Precisely in that primitive condition, however, it was more suited than any other instrument to sustain one tone or one complex of tones above which played a figuration performed by voices or other instruments, particularly voices.[10] Thus it functioned harmonically. With the transition to the pressure keyboard system in the twelfth century and with the increasing melodious movability achieved through special contrivances, the attempt was made to conserve the older function until the double

bourdons were introduced for this purpose. Behr is right
when he directs attention to the fact that (according to
the Cologne *Traktat de organo*)[11] precisely because of
this function many-voiced singing accompanied by the
organ was not allowed to descend beneath the lowest
organ tone. As shown by the name *organizare* for the
creation of many-voiced settings, the organ (and perhaps
also the organistrum) played an important role in the
rationalization of polyvocality.

Since the organ, in contrast to the bagpipe, was tuned
diatonically, it could serve as an important support for
the development of the corresponding tone feeling. On
the other hand, at first it remained purely diatonic
(though it early admitted the b-moll). What was worse,
it long retained pythagorean temperament. Thus it was
unavailable for the production of thirds and sixths. But
in the thirteenth and fully in the fourteenth century a
highly developed coloration together with increasing development occurred.[12] Perhaps the organ directly influenced the figurative polyphony such as prevailed at the
beginning of the *ars nova*.

No instrument of older music had the same kind or
amount of influence as the organ on the evolution of
polyvocality. In the Occident from the beginning only
ecclesiastical use offered a solid basis for the development
of this instrument which became ever more complex after
invention of the pedal and led toward its perfection
through the differentiation of measured musical organization, above all since the early sixteenth century. In a
period without any market, the monastery organization
was the only possible base on which it could prosper.
Thus in the entire early period it remained an instrument
particularly of the Nordic missionary territory, according

to Chrodegang with its strong monasterial foundation, also in the cathedral chapters.[13] Pope John the Eighth asked the Bishop of Freising to send an organ-builder who, as was then the custom, had to function as an organist.

Organ-builders and organists are, at first, either monks or technicians from monasteries or from chapters instructed by monks or canons. After the end of the thirteenth century, when any sizable church obtained an organ, many two of them, organ-building and with it to a considerable degree the practical leadership in development of the tone system lay in the hands of professional secular organ-builders. They not only decided the temperament of the organ, but since vibrations at an impure temperament of the organ are easily determined, they had a hand in bringing about changes far surpassing the problems of temperament in general importance. At the time, the general advance and technical elaboration of this instrument coincides with the great innovations in polyvocal singing which in spite of initial restrictions are unthinkable without the participation of the organ.

Religious Change and the Transformed Function of the Organ

The organ was and remained the representative of ecclesiastical art music, not of the singing of laymen. It was often maintained in earlier times that it was not supposed to accompany congregational singing. Such congregational accompaniment was only very recent.

The Protestants, as in the beginning the Swiss Reformed and almost all ascetic sects, did not banish the organ (precisely because it had served art singing) from the church in the way antique Christendom did the aulos. As Rietschel,[14] too, emphasized, even in the Lutheran church the organ preserved art music under the influence of Luther.[15] It remained, at first, the instrument which supported art music essentially in the old style or which substituted for it. Verses and the text, which was read by the congregation from a hymn book arranged for the organ, alternated with the art productions of the schooled choir. After a brief period of popularity the participation of the congregation itself in the singing so much declined in some as to hardly present a recognizable contrast to the Middle Ages.

The reformed churches were more favorable to congregational singing. Particularly after the French psalm compositions had gained international diffusion, they were opposed to art music. Then, since the end of the sixteenth century the organ was introduced again step by step in most of the reformed churches. On the other hand, a catastrophe to old church music occurred in the Lutheran church with the advance of pietism at the end of the seventeenth century. Only the orthodox retained any considerable amount of art music. It is tragicomic that J. S. Bach's music, which corresponded to his intense religious piety and despite a strict dogmatic relationship bears an unmistakable flavor of pietism, was in his own domicile suspected by the pietists and appreciated by the orthodox.[16]

Thus the function of the organ is relatively new as an instrument which primarily accompanies congregational singing. From olden times it preludes and fills the interludes, the entrance and recession of the congregation, the long ceremony of the communion. In the same fashion as the specifically fervent and religious cachet which organ music means for us today, above all, the sonority of the mixtures and great registers which are supposed to be considered aesthetically and which fundamentally, in spite of Helmholtz, are of barbarian emotional nature.[17]

The organ is an instrument strongly bearing the character of a machine. The person who operates it is rigidly bound by the technical aspects of tone formation, providing him with little liberty to speak his personal language. The organ followed the machine principle in the fact that in the Middle Ages its manipulation required a number of persons, particularly bellows treaders. Machine-like contrivances increasingly substituted for this physical work. In common with the iron forge it faced the problem of creating a continuous supply of air. The twenty-four bellows of the old organ of the cathedral at Magdeburg still needed *Kalkanten.* The organ of the cathedral in Winchester in the tenth century required seventy.[18]

The Piano

The second specifically modern keyboard instrument, the piano, had two technically different historical roots. One was the clavichord, in all probability the invention of a monk.[19]

By increasing the number of strings the clavichord originated from the early medieval monochord, an instrument with one string and a movable bridge which was the basis for the rational tone arrangement of the entire Western civilization. Originally the clavichord had conjunct strings for several tones which, thus, could not be struck simultaneously. It had free strings for only the most important tones. The free strings were gradually increased at the expense of the conjunct strings. With the oldest clavichords, the simultaneous touching of c and e, the third, was impossible.

Its range comprised twenty-two diatonic tones in the fourteenth century (from G to e' including b-flat next to b). At Agricola's time the instrument had been brought to a chromatic scale from A to b'. Its tones, which rapidly died away, encouraged rapid, animated figuration making it an instrument adaptable to art music. The instrument was struck by tangents which limited the sounding part of the string, simultaneously silencing the latter. At the peak of its perfection, the particular sonorous effects of its expressive tone oscillations permitted it to yield before the hammer piano only when a small stratum of musicians and amateurs with delicate ears no longer decided over the fate of musical instruments, but when market situations prevailed and the production of instruments had become capitalistic.

The second source of the piano was the clavicembalo, clavecin, or cembalo, which was derived from the psalterium and English virginal. It differs in many ways. Its strings, one for each tone, were plucked by quills, therefore without capacity for modulation in volume or color, but permitting great freedom and precision of touch.

The clavecin had the same disadvantages mentioned for the organ and similar technical devices were employed in the attempt to correct them. Until the eighteenth century organists were normally the builders of keyboard instruments. Also they were the first creators of piano literature. Since the free touch was favorable to use of the instrument for the reproduction of folk tunes and dances, its specific audience was formed essentially by amateurs, particularly and quite naturally all folk circles tied to home life. In the Middle Ages it was the instrument of monks, later of women led by Queen Elizabeth.[20] As late as 1722 as a recommendation for a new complicated keyboard type it is emphasized that even an experienced woman is able to handle the customary playing of the keyboard.

In the fifteenth and sixteenth centuries the clavecin doubtless participated in the development of music which was melodically and rhythmically transparent. It was one of the mediators for the penetration of popular simple harmonic feeling opposite the polyphonic art music. The theorists built keyboard-like instruments for themselves for experimental purposes.[21] In the sixteenth century, the period of general experimentation with the production of purely tempered instruments for many-voiced compositions, the clavecin was still less important than the lute for vocal accompaniment. However, the cembalo gained territory and became the characteristic instrument for the accompaniment of vocal music, then for the opera.[22] In the seventeenth and eighteenth centuries the conductor sat in the middle of the orchestra. As far as art music is concerned, the instrument remained strongly dependent on the organ in its musical technique until the end of the seventeenth century. Organists and pianists felt themselves to be separated but solitary artists and representatives of harmonic music in contrast, above all, to the string instruments which "could not produce any full harmony," withdrew (with this motivation) in France from the dominance of the king of the viols.

Emancipation of the Piano and Its Emergence as the Instrument of the Middle Classes

French instrumental music showed the influence of the dance, determined by the sociological structure of France. Then, following the example of violin virtuoso performance, musical emancipation of piano music from the organ style of writing was carried out. Chambonnieres may be considered the first creator of specific piano works. Domenico Scarlatti, at the beginning of the eighteenth century, is the first to exploit in virtuoso fashion the peculiar sonorous effects of the instrument.[23] Piano virtuosity developed hand in hand with a heavy harpsichord industry which was based on the demand of orchestras and amateurs. Continued development led on to the last great technical changes of the instrument and its typification. The first great builder of harpsichords (around 1600 the family Ruckers in Belgium)[24] operated like a manufacturer creating individual instruments commissioned by specific consumers (orchestras and patricians) and thus in very manifold adaptation to all possible special needs quite in the manner of the organ.

The development of the hammer piano occurred by stages partly in Italy (Christoferi) partly in Germany. Inventions made in Italy remained unexploited there. Italian culture (until the threshold of the present) remained alien to the indoor culture of the Nordic Europe.

Italian ideals lacked the influence of the culture of the bourgeois-like home. They retained the ideal of *a capella* singing and the opera. The arias of the opera supplied the popular demand for easily comprehensible and singable tunes.

The center of gravity of the production and technical

improvement of the piano lies in the musically most broadly organized country, Saxony. The bourgeois-like musical culture derived from the *Kantorelen* virtuosi and builders of instruments proceeded hand in hand with an intense interest in the orchestra of the count. Beyond this it underwent continuous improvement and popularization. In the foreground of interest was the possibility of muffling and increasing the volume of the tone, the sustaining of the tone and the beautiful perfection of the chords played in the form of arpeggios at any tone distance. In contrast to these advantages was the disadvantage (especially according to Bach) of deficient freedom, in contrast to the harpsichord and clavichord, in playing fast passages. The removal of this disadvantage was of major concern.

In place of the tapping touch of the keyboard instruments of the sixteenth century, beginning with the organ a rational fingering technique was in progress, soon extended to the harpsichord. This presented the hands working into each other, the fingers crossing over one another. To our conception this was still tortured enough. Eventually the Bachs placed fingering technique, one would like to say, on a "physiological tonal" basis by a rational use of the thumb.[25] In antiquity the highest virtuoso achievements occurred on the aulos. Now the violin and, above all, the piano presented the most difficult tasks.

The great artists of modern piano music, Johann Sebastian and Philipp Emanuel Bach were still neutral toward the hammer piano. J. S. Bach in particular wrote an important part of his best work for the old types of instruments, the clavichord and harpsichord. These were weaker and more intimate than the piano and with respect to sonority calculated for more delicate ears. Only the internationally famous virtuosity of Mozart and the increasing need of music publishers and of concert managers to satisfy the large music consumption of the mass market brought the final victory of the hammer piano.

In the eighteenth century the piano-builders, above all, the German, were still artisans who collaborated and experimented physically (like Silbermann).[26] Machine-made mass production of the piano occurred first in England (Broadwood) then in America (Steinway) where first-rate iron could be pressed into construction of the frame. Moreover, iron helped overcome the numerous purely climatic difficulties that could affect adoption of the piano. Incidentally, climatic difficulties also stood in the way of adoption of the piano in the tropics. By the beginning of the nineteenth century the piano had become a standard commercial object produced for stock.

The wild competitive struggle of the factories played a role in the development of the instrument. So, too, did the virtuosi with the special modern devices of the press, exhibitions, and finally analogous to salesman techniques of breweries, of the building of concert halls, of the instrument factories of their own (with us, above all, those of the Berliner). These forces brought about that technical perfection of the instrument which alone could satisfy the ever increasing technical demands of the composers. The older instruments were already no match for Beethoven's later creations.

Meanwhile, orchestra works were made accessible for home use only in the form of piano transcriptions. In Chopin a first rank composer was found who restricted himself entirely to the piano. Finally in Liszt the intimate skill of the great virtuoso elicited from the instrument all that had finally been concealed of expressive possibilities.

The unshakable modern position of the piano rests upon

the universality of its usefulness for domestic appropria-
tion of almost all treasures of music literature, upon the
immeasurable fullness of its own literature and finally on
its quality as a universal accompanying and schooling instrument. In its function as a school instrument, it displaced the antique kithara, the monochord, the primitive
organ, and the barrel-lyre of the monastic schools. As an
accompanying instrument it displaced the aulos of antiquity, the organ, and the primitive string instruments
of the Middle Ages and the lute of the Renaissance. As
an amateur instrument of the upper classes it displaced
the kithara of antiquity, the harp, of the North, and the
lute of the sixteenth century. Our exclusive education
toward modern harmonic music is represented quite essentially by it.

Even the negative aspects of the piano are important.
Temperament takes from our ears some of the delicacy
which gave the decisive flavor to the melodious refinement of ancient music culture. Until the sixteenth century the training of singers in the Occident took place on
the monochord. According to Zarline, the singers trained
in this manner attempted to reintroduce perfect temperament. Today their training occurs almost exclusively on
the piano. And today, at least in our latitudes, tone formation and schooling of string instruments is practised
from the beginning at the piano. It is clear that delicate
hearing capacity possible with training by means of instruments in pure temperament cannot be reached. The
notoriously greater imperfection in the intonation of
Nordic as compared to Italian singers must be caused
by it.

The idea of building pianos with twenty-four keys in
the octave, as suggested by Helmholtz, is not promising

for economic reasons. The building of the piano is conditioned by the mass market. It is the peculiar nature of the piano to be a middle-class home instrument. As the organ requires a giant indoor space the piano requires a moderately large indoor space to display its best enchantments. All the successes of the modern piano virtuosi cannot basically change the fact that the instrument in its independent appearances in the large concert hall is involuntarily compared with the orchestra and obviously found to be too light.

Therefore it is no accident that the representatives of pianistic culture are Nordic peoples, climatically housebound and home-centered in contrast to the South. In southern Europe the cultivation of middle-class home comforts was restricted by climatic and historical factors. The piano was invented there but did not diffuse quickly as in the North. Nor did it rise to an equivalent position as a significant piece of middle-class furniture.

Notes

Index

Notes

INTRODUCTION

1. First published by Drei Masken Verlag (Munich, 1921); republished as an appendix to Volume II of Weber's *Wirtschaft und Gesellschaft* (Tübingen: J. C. B. Mohr, 1921); reprinted in the edition of 1924 and in that of 1956. The 1956 edition has textual corrections by Johannes Winckelmann.

2. Marianne Weber, *Max Weber: Ein Lebensbild* (Tübingen: J. C. B. Mohr, 1925); for an excellent intellectual biography see H. H. Gerth and C. Wright Mills, *From Max Weber: Essays in Sociology* (New York: Oxford University Press, 1946).

3. Max Weber, *Die protestantische Ethik und der Geist des Kapitalismus*, in *Archiv für Socialwissenschaft und Socialpolitik*, Vols. XX, XXI (1904–1905); tr. by Talcott Parsons (New York: Scribner, 1930).

4. A bibliography of Weber's writings is contained in Marianne Weber's *Max Weber: Ein Lebensbild.*

5. The most complete review of his basic concepts appears in Part I of Max Weber's *Wirtschaft und Gesellschaft,* 4th ed. (Tübingen, 1956), pp. 1–30. This has been translated by A. M. Henderson and Talcott Parsons in *Max Weber: The Theory of Social and Economic Organization* (New York: Oxford University Press, 1947).

6. This type of sociology has been called "social behaviorism." There are other kinds of sociological theory that violently reject this, asserting it to be a kind of social atomism. Contem-

porary sociological functionalism, for example, assumes that social life is found only in systems.

7. The famous typology of action erected on this foundation described these various kinds of actions as *zweckrational, wertrational,* affective, and traditional. See *The Theory of Social and Economic Organization,* p. 114.

8. See *ibid.,* p. 118.

9. See Weber's formulation in "Science as a Vocation" in Gerth and Mills, *op. cit.,* pp. 139 ff.

10. See the introduction to *The Protestant Ethic* (Parson's translation, pp. 13 ff.) for a brief summary of Weber's views on these matters.

11. Paul H. Hindemith, *The Craft of Musical Composition* (New York: Associated Musical Publishers, 1945), p. 164.

12. See E. Clements, *Introduction to the Study of Indian Music* (London: Longmans, Green, 1913), pp. 11–14.

13. Henry George Farmer, *A History of Arabian Music* (London: Luzac, 1929), pp. 205 f.

14. Clements, *op. cit.,* Appendix E, pp. 100–101.

15. Carl Stumpf, *Die Anfänge der Musik* (Leipzig, 1911).

16. Curt Sachs, *The History of Musical Instruments* (New York: Norton, 1940).

17. Curt Sachs, *The Rise of Music in the Ancient World: East and West* (New York: Norton, 1943).

18. This is the literary appellation of the instrument shaped like the mortar. Its popular name is ch'ing. It is struck with a wooden hammer. When used at religious ceremonies it is placed in a kind of silken purse richly ornamented with rare fish scales.

19. Oldest form of bowed instrument known in England, dating to four hundred years before Christ. Ancestor of the violin and descendant of the Irish cruit.

CHAPTER I

1. The pythagorean comma is the difference between the twelfth, fifth, and seventh octave above a given note in a mathematically perfect scale. It is different from the comma syntonum or comma of Didymos. When the scale is mathe-

matically perfect, the interval between one and two is a major tone and between two and three a minor. The majors contain nine commas and the minors eight. A Didymos comma is the difference between a major and a minor.

2. For his discussion of the dominant seventh chord see Hermann L. F. Helmholtz, *On the Sensations of Tone*, 2nd rev. ed. by Alexander F. Ellis, with a new Introduction by Henry Margenau (New York: Dover Publications, Inc., 1954), pp. 341 ff.

3. *Ibid.*, p. 355.

4. Jean Philippe Rameau, *Traité de l'harmonie reduite à ses principes naturels* (1722).

5. Helmholtz, *op. cit.*, p. 356.

6. Sig. A. Basevis, *Introduction à un nouveau système d'harmonie* (Florence, 1955).

7. "Modern" is taken in the sense of Wagnerian music. See Ernst Kurth, *Die romantische Harmonik und ihre Krise in Wagners "Tristan"* (Leipzig, 1920).

CHAPTER II

1. Moritz Hauptmann, *Die Natur der Harmonik und Metrik* (Leipzig, 1853), pp. 26 ff.

2. Johann Phil. Kirnberger, *Die Kunst des reinen Satzes in der Musik* (1774–1779); Hugo Riemann, *Geschichte des Musiktheorie im IX–XIX Jahrhundert*, 2d ed. (Berlin: Max Hesse, 1920), pp. 476 ff.

3. Helmholtz, *op. cit.*, pp. 77, 545 ff.

4. With respect to Ernst Florens Friedrich Chladni's writings, compare his *Akustik* (1802) and his *Kurze Uebersicht der Schall- und Klanglehre* (1827).

5. Helmholtz, *op. cit.*, p. 257.

6. Ludwig Erk and Frank Magnus Boehme, *Deutscher Liederhort*, 3 vols. (1893–1894).

7. Oscar Fleischer, "Zur vergleichenden Liedforschung," *Sammelbände der Internationalen Musikgesellschaft*, III (1901–1902), 185 ff. Of the many recent studies, the article by Bruno Nettl should be mentioned: "Change in Folk and Primitive Music: A Survey of Methods and Studies," *Journal*

of American Musicological Society, VIII (Summer, 1955), 101 ff.

8. Basic information on Jewish music and liturgy may be found in the following works by Abraham Zebi Idelsohn: *Jewish Music in its Historical Development* (New York: Holt, 1929); *Jewish Liturgy and its Development* (New York: Holt, 1932); *Thesaurus of Oriental Hebrew Melodies,* 10 vols. (Berlin: Harz, 1922–1932).

9. Helmholtz, *op. cit.,* p. 556.

10. *Ibid.,* pp. 518, 522.

11. *Ibid.,* p. 517 c, d.

12. Frances Densmore, "Chippewa Music," *Bureau of American Ethnology Bulletin* No. 45 (1910), 53 (1913).

13. Helmholtz, *op. cit.,* p. 526.

14. *Ibid.,* p. 518, nos. 96, 97–102.

15. *Ibid.,* pp. 200 ff.

16. Giovanni Domenico Mansi, *Sacrorum Conciliorum Collectio,* Vol. XII (1766), col. 399; A. W. Haddan and W. Stubbs, *Councils and Ecclesiastical Documents,* III (1871), 367.

17. Helmholtz, *op. cit.,* p. 260.

18. Frances Densmore, "The Melodic Formation of Indian Songs," *Journal of Washington Academy of Sciences,* XVIII (1928), 395–408.

19. For Helmholtz, *op. cit.,* pp. 190 ff.

20. Frances Densmore, "The Music of the American Indians," *The Overland Monthly,* March, 1905, pp. 230–34; "Scale Formation in Primitive Music," *American Anthropologist,* n.s., XI (1909), 1–12; "Chippewa Music," *Bureau of American Ethnology Bulletin* No. 45 (1910).

21. Helmholtz, *op. cit.,* pp. 186 ff.

22. *Ibid.,* pp. 518, 526.

23. *Ibid.,* p. 262 b.

24. See the examples of Greek music available in modern transcriptions by Gustav Reese, *Music in the Middle Ages,* (New York: Norton, 1940), p. 48, note 90.

25. Helmholtz, *op. cit.,* pp. 262, 263.

26. Reese, *loc. cit.*

27. Curt Sachs, "Ueber eine bosnische Doppelflöte," *Sam-*

melbände der Internationalen Musikgesellschaft, IX (1907–1908), 313 f.

28. Raphael Georg Kiesewetter, *Die Musik der Araber nach Originalquellen dargestellt* (Leipzig, 1842); Guillaume André Villoteau, "Descriptions des instruments de musique des orientaux," in his *Description de l'Egypte* (1809).

29. Père Collangettes, "Etude sur la musique arabe," *Journal Asiatique* (1904–1906).

30. See J. Murray Barbour, *Tuning and Temperament* (East Lansing, Mich., 1951).

31. See Henry George Farmer, *A History of Arabian Music* (London: Luzac, 1929), pp. 118 ff.

32. R. G. Kiesewetter, *Die Musik der Araber* (Leipzig, 1842); Helmholtz, *op. cit.,* pp. 264, 285, 525.

33. A. H. Fox Strangways, *The Music of Hindostan* (Oxford: Clarendon Press, 1914), pp. 118 ff.

34. John Hazedel Levis, *The Foundations of Chinese Musical Art* (Peiping: Henri Vetch, 1936), p. 91.

35. Helmholtz, *op. cit.,* p. 229 c.

36. Heinz Trefzger, "Ueber das K'in, seine Geschichte, seine Technik, seine Notation, und seine Philsophie," *Schweizerische Musikzeitung,* LXXXVIII (1948), 81 ff.

37. Helmholtz, *op. cit.,* pp. 262 c, 263 a, 228 e.

CHAPTER III

1. Reese, *Music in the Middle Ages,* p. 48, note 90.

2. Helmholtz, *op. cit.,* Ch. XIV, pp. 250–90.

3. Sir John Stainer maintains that harmony had its origins in melody. See his *Theory of Harmony, Founded on the Tempered Scale* (1871).

4. E. Fischer, "Patagonische Musik," *Anthropos,* Vol. III (1908); Robert Lehmann-Nitsche, "Patagonische Gesänge und Musikbogen," *ibid.*

5. For specific works by these authorities see the bibliography in Jaap Kunst's *Ethno-Musicology* (The Hague: Martinus Nijhoff, 1955), pp. 65 ff.

6. Helmholtz, *op. cit.,* p. 243 b.

7. Max Wertheimer, "Musik der Wedda," *Sammelbände der Internationalen Musikgesellschaft,* XI (1909), 300 ff.

8. Thrasybulus Georgiades, *Vers und Sprache: Musik und Sprache* (Berlin, 1954).

9. Father Witte, "Lieder und Gesänge der Ewe Neger," *Anthropos,* Vol. I (1906).

10. Otto Crusius, *Die delphischen Hymnen. Untersuchungen über Texte und Melodien* (Göttingen, 1894).

11. Witte, in *Anthropos,* Vol. I.

12. Frances Densmore, "The Melodic Formation of Indian Songs," *Journal of Washington Academy of Sciences,* XVIII (1928), 395-408; "What Intervals do Indians Sing?" *American Anthropologist,* XXXI (1929), 271-76.

13. Wertheimer, *loc. cit.*

14. E. Fischer, in *Anthropos,* Vol. III. On the musical bow see also Belfour, *The Natural History of the Musical Bow* (1899).

15. Reese, *loc. cit.*

16. Erich von Hornbostel, "Wanyamwesi-Gesänge," *Anthropos,* Vol. IV (1909).

17. Jules Combarieu, *La musique et la magie: Etude sur les origines populaires de l'art musical, son influence et sa fonction dans les sociétés* (Paris, 1909).

18. Albert Howard, "The Aulos or Tibia," *Harvard Studies in Philology,* Vol. IV (1893). A modern standard work is Kathleen Schlesinger's *The Greek Aulos* (London, 1939).

19. Weber, it may be noted, uses "practical" as a term to refer both to everyday conduct, as above when he referred to magical musical formulae as practical, and to instrumental requirements, as in the present context.

20. Helmholtz, *op. cit.,* Ch. XVI, pp. 310-30, 514 ff.

21. *Ibid.,* p. 242 a.

22. *Ibid.,* p. 217 a.

23. For Byzantine church modes see H. J. W. Tillyard, *Byzantine Music and Hymnography* (1923); Egon Wellesz, *Byzantinische Musik* (1927).

24. K. Keworkian, "Die armenische Kirchenmusik," *Sammelbände der Internationalen Musikgesellschaft,* Vol. I; also

Egon Wellesz, "Die armenische Messe und ihre Musik," *Peters Jahrbuch* (1920).

25. For a new comparative study of Christian and Jewish liturgy and music see Erich Werner, *The Sacred Bridge* (New York: Columbia Univ. Press, 1956).

26. Erich M. von Hornbostel, "Melodie und Skala," *Peters Jahrbuch* (1913).

27. On pseudo-Aristotelian theories see Ch. Edmond Henrie de Coussemaker, *Scriptores de musica medii aevi*, 4 vols. (1864–1876); also Carl Stumpf, *Die pseudo-aristotelischen Probleme über die Musik* (1897).

CHAPTER IV

1. Helmholtz, *op. cit.*, p. 267 c.

2. Stumpf, *Die pseudo-aristotelischen Probleme über die Musik*.

3. Helmholtz, *op. cit.*, p. 278 d.

4. *Ibid.*, p. 266 b, c.

5. Camille Saint-Saëns, "Lyres et cithares en Lavignac," *Encyclopédie de la musique*, I (1912), 538 ff.

6. For a discussion of Aristotle's explanation of the *mese* see Helmholtz, *op. cit.*, pp. 240–41.

7. Kiesewetter, *Die Musik der Araber nach Originalquellen dargestellt;* Villouteau, "Description des instruments de musique des orientaux," in *Descriptions de l'Egypte*.

8. Père Collangettes, "Etude sur la musique arabe," *Journal Asiatique* (1904–1906).

9. For references to the following discussion see Helmholtz, *op. cit.*, pp. 282–84.

10. Guido d'Arezzo, *Regulae de ignotu cantu* and *Epistola Michaeli monachi de ignotu cantu directa*, in Martin Gerbert, *Scriptores ecclesiastici de musica sacra*, Vol. II (1784); trans. of *Epistola* in Oliver Strunk, *Source Readings in Music History* (New York: Norton, 1950), pp. 121 ff.

11. The text of the St. John hymn reads:

Ut queant laxis
resonare fibris

mira gestorum
famuli tuorum
solve polluti
labii reatum,
Sancte Johannes.

As translated in Reese, *Music of the Middle Ages* (p. 150), this reads: "That with enfranchised voices thy servants may be able to proclaim the wonders of thy deeds, remove the sins of (their) polluted lips, O holy John."

12. The design of the solmisation scale shown here is taken from August Wilhelm Ambros, *Geschichte der Musik,* 2nd ed. (Leipzig, 1881), p. 174.

ee					la	
dd				la	sol	
cc				sol	fa	
bb				fa	mi	
aa			la	mi	re	
g			sol	re	ut...	hexachordum durum superacutum
f			fa	ut.......		hexachordum molle acutum
e		la	mi			
d	la	sol	re			
c	sol	fa	ut..........			hexachordum naturale acutum
b	fa	mi				
a	la	mi	re			
G	sol	re	ut..............			hexachordum durum acutum
F	fa	ut..................				hexachordum molle grave
E	la	mi				
D	sol	re				
C	fa	ut......................				hexachordum naturale grave
B	mi					
A	re..........................					hexachordum grave

13. As recently by A. H. Fox-Strangways, *The Music of Hindostan* (Oxford, 1914).

14. Reese, *op. cit.*

15. François August Gevaert, *Histoire et théorie de la musique de l'antiquité,* 2 vols. (Ghent: Annoot-Braeckmann, 1875–1881); *Traité d'harmonie théoretique et pratique,* 2 vols. (Paris: Lemoine, 1905–1907); Gevaert and J. C. Vollgraff (eds.) *Les problemes musicaux d'Aristotle* (Ghent: Hoste, 1903).

16. Hugo Riemann, *Handbuch der Musikgeschichte* (Leipzig, 1901), I, 238 ff.

17. Paul Marquard (ed.) *Die harmonischen Fragmente des Aristoxenos* (Berlin: Weidmann, 1868).

18. Weber probably refers to the second Delphic hymn. A good example is given in Sachs, *The Rise of Music in the Ancient World;* also in Otto Gombosi, *Tonarten und Stimmungen der antiken Musik* (1939), pp. 124 ff.

CHAPTER V

1. Helmholtz, *op. cit.*, p. 556; also Frederick William Verney, *Notes on Siamese Musical Instruments* (London, 1885).

2. For Bantu music see Percival R. Kirby, "The Recognition and Practical Use of the Harmonics of Stretched Strings by the Bantu of South Africa," *Bantu Studies*, Vol. VI (1832); "Some Problems of Primitive Harmony, with Special Reference to Bantu Practice," *South African Journal of Science*, Vol. XXIII (1926); "A Study of Negro Harmony," *Musical Quarterly*, Vol. XVI (1930).

3. Eduard August Grell, *Aufsätze und Gutachten über Musik,* ed. by Johann Gottfried Heinrich Bellermann (Berlin, 1887).

4. An exhaustive bibliography of Bellermann's publications appears in Dietrich Sasse, *Familie Bellermann, Musik in Geschichte und Gegenwart* (Cassel, 1949–1951), I, 1606 f.

5. Rudolph Westphal, *Die Fragmente und Lehrsätze der griechischen Rhythmiker* (1861); *Geschichte der alten und mittelalterlichen Musik* (Breslau, 1864); Sachs, *The Rise of Music in the Ancient World,* pp. 256 ff.

6. For a comprehensive discussion of polyphony in ancient cultures see Sachs, *op. cit.,* pp. 48 ff., 289 ff.

7. On the problem of many-voiced music in Hellas see Ellis' footnote to Helmholtz, *op. cit.,* p. 251 a.

8. Manfred Bukofzer, *"Sumer is icumen in": A Revision* (Berkeley: Univ. of Calif. Publications in Music, No. 2, 1944), p. 79.

9. Weber refers to the innumerable contrapuntal settings of

German *Lieder* during the sixteenth century composed by Flemish and German authors such as Isaac, Senfl, Hofhaimer, and Heinrich Finck.

10. On the rules of polyvocal progression as developed since the twelfth century see Riemann, *Geschichte der Musiktheorie* (Leipzig, 1898); also John F. Spratt, "Contrapuntal Theory of the Fourteenth and Fifteenth Centuries from the *Geschichte der Musiktheorie* by Hugo Riemann," *Studies in Music History and Theory* (Tallahassee, 1955), pp. 41 ff.

11. E. M. von Hornbostel, "Phonographierte isländische Zwiegesänge," *Deutsche Islandforschung* (Breslau, 1933).

12. The interval of the tritone is touched in the first three measures of the first Delphic hymn as quoted by Sachs, *op. cit.*, p. 240.

13. Weber refers to mass and motet compositions of composers of the Burgundian and Flemish schools—Dufay, Okeghem, Obrecht, etc.

14. Henricus Glareanus, *Glareani Dodechachordon* (Basel, 1547), ed. and tr. by Peter Bohn, *Publikation älterer praktischer und theoretischer Musikwerke*, Vol. XVI (Leipzig, 1888).

15. Reese, *Music in the Middle Ages*, pp. 360 ff.

16. Sachs, *op. cit.*, pp. 48 ff., 289 ff.

17. Riemann, *Handbuch der Musikgeschichte*, 3rd rev. ed. (Leipzig, 1923), I, 120 ff.

18. Jaap Kunst, *Music in Java, Its History, Its Theory and Its Technique*, 2 vols. (The Hague, 1949); also Curt Sachs, *Der Gamelan. 50. Jahresbericht der Staatlichen Akademischen Hochschule für Musik in Berlin* (1929), pp. 230 ff.

19. Erich von Hornbostel, "Ueber die Musik der Kubu," in B. Haben, *Die Orang-Kubu auf Sumatra* (Frankfurt-Main, 1908); repr. in *Sammelbände für vergleichende Musikwissenschaft*, I (1922), 359 ff.

20. Sh. Isawa, *Collection of Koto Music* (Tokyo, 1888, 1913).

21. Helmholtz, *op. cit.*, p. 243 b.

22. A. Dirr, "25 georgische Volkslieder," *Anthropos*, Vol. V (1910).

23. Hucbald, *De Harmonica Institutionis*, in Gerbert, *op. cit.*, I, 104 ff.; anon., *Musica enchiriadis, ibid.*, pp. 18 ff.

24. Erich von Hornbostel, "Ueber Mehrstimmigkeit in der aussereuropäischen Musik," *III, Kongress der Internationalen Musikgesellschaft* (Vienna, 1909), pp. 298 ff.

25. Wilhelm Heintz, "Musikinstrumente und Phonograme des Ost-Mbam-Landes," in F. and M. Thorbecke, *Im Hochland vom Mittelkamerun* (Vienna, 1909), pp. 298 ff.

26. Charles Emile Ruelle, *Collection des auteurs grecs relatifs à la musique Alypius et Gaudence* (1895); A. Samojloff, *Die alpius'schen Reihen der altgriechischen Tonbezeichnung*, *Archiv für Musikwissenschaft*, Vol. I (1924).

27. Oscar Fleischer, *Neumenstudien. Abhandlung über mittelalterliche Gesangstobschriften*, 3 vols. (Leipzig, 1895–1897); Hugo Riemann, *Studien zur Geschichte der Notenschrift* (1878); Antone Fr. J. Thibaut, *Ueber Reinheit der Tonkunst*, 2nd rev. ed. (Heidelberg, 1826); Oscar von Riesemann, *Die Notationen des altrussischen Kirchengesanges* (1907).

28. Athanasius Kircher, *Musurgia universalis sive ars magna consoni et dissoni*, 2 vols. (Rome, 1650).

29. Johannes Wolf, *Geschichte der Mensuralnotation von 1250–1460*, 3 vols. (Leipzig: Brietkopf und Gaertel, 1904).

30. Fr. Caffi, *Storia della musica . . . di S. Marco in Venezia*, 2 vols. (Venice, 1854–1855).

31. Franz Xavier Haberl, "Die römische Schola Cantorum und die päpstlichen Kapellsänger," *Vierteljahrschrift für Musikwissenschaft*, Vol. III (1887).

32. With the Flemish school Weber refers to both Burgundian and Flemish schools.

33. Raphael Georg Kiesewetter (Edler von Wiesenbrun), *Die Verdienste der Niederländer um die Tonkunst* (1826).

CHAPTER VI

1. For selections of Peter Wagner's writings on the Gregorian chant see Reese, *Music in the Middle Ages*, p. 439; Hans Joachim Moser, *Musik Lexikon*, 4th rev. ed. (Hamburg, 1955); for the writings of François Auguste Gevaert see *Les Origines du chant liturgique de l'église latine* (Ghent, 1890) and *La*

mélopée antique dans le chant de l'église latine (Ghent, 1895–1896).

2. See particularly Manuel Bryennios, *Harmonics,* in J. Wallis, *Opera math.* (1699).

3. F. Gascué, "Origen de la musica popular vascogada," *Revista int. de Estudios Vascos* (1913).

4. Father Witte, in *Anthropos,* Vol. I (1906).

5. William H. Grattan Flood, *The Story of the Bagpipe* (London, 1911).

6. Helmholtz, *op. cit.,* pp. 77, 545 ff.

7. *Ibid.,* pp. 280–84, 515–17.

8. *Ibid.,* p. 517 b.

9. See Henry George Farmer, *The Music and Musical Instruments of the Arab* (London: F. Salvador Daniel, 1915); "The Influence of Al-Farabi's Ihsa' al' ulum (De Scientiis) on the Writers on Music in Western Europe," *Journal of the Royal Asiatic Society* (1931), pp. 349 ff.; *Al Farabi's Arabic Latin Writings on Music* (Glasgow, 1934).

10. Helmholtz, *op. cit.,* p. 517 b.

11. Heinz Trefzger, "Ueber das K'in, seine Geschichte, seine Technik, seine Notation und seine Philosophie," *Schweizerische Musikzeitung,* LXXXVIII (1948), 81 ff.; R. M. Marks, "The Music and Musical Instruments of Ancient China," *Musical Quarterly,* Vol. XVIII (1933).

12. Helmholtz, *op. cit.,* p. 556 a.

13. *Ibid.,* pp. 518 d, 522 b. Compare also references in note 18, Chapter V, and Manfred F. Bukofzer, "The Evolution of Javanese Tone Systems," *Papers Read at the International Congress of Musicology* (New York, 1939).

14. Carl Stumpf, "Tonsystem und Musik der Siamesen," *Beiträge zur Akustik und Musikwissenschaft,* repr. in *Sammelbände für vergleichende Musikwissenschaft,* Vol. I (1922).

15. On the holiness of numbers see the discussions of Jules Combarieu: *La musique et la magie* (Paris, 1909); *Histoire de la musique* (Paris, 1913), I, 39.

16. Carl Philipp Emanuel Bach, *Essay on the True Art of Playing Keyboard Instruments,* ed. and tr. by William J. Mitchell (New York: Norton, 1949).

17. Helmholtz, *op. cit.*, p. 356 b; R. de Récy, "Rameau et les encyclopédistes," *Revue des deux mondes* (1886); A. R. Oliver, *The Encyclopedists as Critics of Music* (New York: Columbia University Press, 1947).

CHAPTER VII

1. Wantzloeben, *Das Monochord als Instrument und als System* (Halle, 1911).
2. Curt Sachs, *Reallexikon der Musikinstrumente* (Berlin, 1913).
3. G. Hart, *The Violin* (1875); A. Vidal, *Les Instruments à l'archet* (1876); Carl Engel, *Researches into the Early History of the Violin Family* (1883).
4. Edward Jones, *Musical Relics of the Welsh Bards* (1794); Francis William Galpin, *Old English Instruments of Music, Their History and Character* (London, 1911).
5. T. Gwyn Jones, "Bardism and Romance," *Transactions of the Honorable Society of Cymmrodorion* (1913–1914).
6. Sebastian Virdung, *Music getutscht* (Basel, 1511), ed. by Leo Schrade (Cassel: Baerenreiter, 1931).
7. By Renaissance Weber here means the early baroque period.
8. Kathleen Schlesinger, "Researches into the Origins of the Organs of the Ancients," *Sammelbände der Internationalen Musikgesellschaft*, II (1900–1901), 167 ff.
9. J. W. Warman, "The Hydraulic Organ of the Ancients," *Proceedings of the Music Association* (1903–1904); Francis W. Galpin, "Notes on a Hydraulis," *The Reliquary* (1904); Charles Macleau, "The Principle of the Hydraulic Organ," *Sammelbände der Internationalen Musikgesellschaft*, VI (1905), 183 ff.; R. Tannery, "L'Invention de l'hydraulis," *Revue des études grecques*, Vol. XII (1908).
10. Conrad Amelin (ed.), "Fundamentum organisandi Magister Conradi Paumans," *Locheimer Liederbuch*.
11. Riemann, *Gesichte der Musiktheorie* (1898), pp. 20 ff.
12. B. A. Wallner, *Buxheimer Orgelbuch*, fac, reprint in *Documenta Musicologica* (Cassel: Baerenreiter, 1955).
13. See Dom Anselm Hughes, *Early Medieval Music up to*

1300 (New York: Oxford University Press, 1954), pp. 81, 100.

14. Georg Christian Rietschel, *Die Aufgaben der Orgel im evangelischen Gottesdienst bis ins 18. Jahrhundert* (1893).

15. Weber refers to Luther's interest in Josquin's and Senff's music. Emphasis on art music can also be seen in Johann Walther's four- and five-part chorale settings.

16. Hans David and Arthur Mendel, *The Bach Reader* (New York: Norton, 1945), p. 24.

17. Helmholtz, *op. cit.*, p. 206 c.

18. Bernhard Engelke, *Musikgeschichte in Magdeburger Dom bis 1631* (1913); Wackerbarth, *Music and the Anglo-Saxons*, pp. 12–15.

19. Carl Auerbach, *Die deutsche Klavichordkunst des 18. Jahrhunderts* (Cassel: Baerenreiter, 1930); H. Neupert, *Das Klavichord* (Cassel: Baerenreiter, 1949).

20. Margaret H. Glyn, "The National School of Virginal Music in Elizabethan Times," *Proceedings of the Music Association*, Vol. XLIII (1917).

21. A famous instrument of this sort was that of the Renaissance theorist Nicolog Vincentino who defends it in his *L'antica musica ridotta alla moderna prattica* (1555).

22. Weber is referring to the beginning of the seventeenth century.

23. Ralph Kirkpatrick, *Domenico Scarlatti* (Princeton, N.J., and London, 1953).

24. E. Closson, *La facture des instruments de musique en Belgique* (Brussels, 1935).

25. David and Mendel, *op. cit.*, pp. 306 ff.

26. A. Mooser, *Gottfried Silbermann* (Langensalza, 1857).

Index

ABRAHAM, O., 34
Acoustical laws: pythagorean theory of, xxvii
Admiralty Islands, music of: use of second parallels, 81
Agoge peripheres: use of b-flat string in modulation, 56
Al Farabi, 95, 96
Amanites, music of: pentatonic basis, 15, 16
Amati family, 110
Arabic Music: use of fourths and fifths, xli, 47, 52, 56, 62, 64, 96; use of integral 7, 12–13; scale freedom, 22; development of theory, 26–29; exclusion of use of near-lying tones, 42; range of instruments, 43; use of minor second, 49; influence on Javanese music, 58; loss of notation, 84; restriction of harmony in Asia Minor, 93; as drill ground of musical experimentalism, 94
Archimedes, 112
Archytas of Tarentum, 24, 30
Aristophanes, 24
Aristotle, 70
Aristoxenus, 64, 98
Armenian music: recitative-like final cadence, 46

BACH, Johann Sebastian, xlvi, 7, 44, 69, 100, 116
Bach, Philipp Emanuel, 121
Bagpipe: primitive instrument of cattle breeders, 93. *See also* Organ
Bamboo flute: as key instrument of Chinese, 27
Bantu Negroes, music of: legends and recitations, 67; use of fourth and fifth parallels, 81; use of thirds in instrumental interludes, 82
Bards: influence on development of strings, 106–8
Basevis, Sig. A., 8
Beethoven, Ludwig van, 122
Bellerman, Johann Gottfried, 69
Bryennies, 26, 37
Byzantine music: use of fourths and fifths, xl, 52; use of integral 7, 13; scale freedom, 22; tone progressions, 37; conversion of church modes into type of octave, 45; use of repercussion interval, 49, 50; transposition devices, 58; modulation, 73; use of notation, 84; splitting of semitones, 89; use of organ as festival instrument, 112

141